Audrey Deane has a BSc.(Hons) degree in Food Science and Nutrition. Coupled with more than twenty years of experience in the food retail sector, Audrey has acquired many skills ranging from food production and global ingredient procurement to recipe development, food writing and nutrition. Her intimate knowledge of ingredients enables her to get the best out of cooking your own food.

You might also like

The Healthy Slow Cooker Cookbook
Low-Carb Slow Cooker
Slow Cooker Family Classics
The Keto Slow Cooker
Slow Cooker: for Less
The Sugar-Free Family Cookbook
The Healthy Halogen Cookbook
Perfect Baking with Your Halogen Oven
Halogen Cooking for Two
The Everyday Halogen Family Cookbook
The Everyday Halogen Oven Cookbook
Eating to Beat Type 2 Diabetes

the
SLOW COOKER
cookbook

AUDREY DEANE

ROBINSON

ROBINSON

First published in Great Britain in 2013 by Spring Hill,
an imprint of Constable & Robinson Ltd

This edition published in Great Britain in 2022 by Robinson

1 3 5 7 9 10 8 6 4 2

A CIP catalogue record for this book
is available from the British Library.

ISBN 978-1-47214-703-5

Designed by Ian Hughes, Mousemat Design Limited
Printed in Slovenia by DZS Grafik

Papers used by Robinson are from well-managed forests
and other responsible sources

Robinson
An imprint of
Little, Brown Book Group
Carmelite House
50 Victoria Embankment
London EC4Y 0DZ

An Hachette UK Company
www.hachette.co.uk

www.littlebrown.co.uk

NOTE: The material contained in this book is set out in good faith for general
guidance and no liability can be accepted for loss or expense incurred as a result of relying in
particular circumstances on statements made in the book. Laws and regulations are complex
and liable to change, and readers should check the current position with relevant
authorities before making personal arrangements.

How To Books are published by Robinson, an imprint of Little, Brown Book Group.
We welcome proposals from authors who have first-hand experience of their subjects. Please
set out the aims of your book, its target market and its suggested contents in an email to
HowTo@littlebrown.co.uk

Acknowledgements

I would like to personally thank the wonderful people who have contributed to this recipe book throughout its development. From insightful initial research and thorough recipe testing through to lending crockery and tablecloths for some great photography by my brother. This book has piqued the interest of many of my family and friends and their continued encouragement and interest has been invaluable in achieving the final result of a truly family-focused slow cooker recipe book. Many underused slow cookers have very definitely emerged from cupboards and made a welcome return to the kitchen worktop. Thank you all.

Disclaimer

The temperatures and timings listed in the recipes are guides as slow cookers can vary, so get to know your slow cooker. Older slow cookers or very basic ones can often cook a little hotter than they should. If your slow cooker is bubbling away and evaporating liquid, it may be best to cook on low rather than high and opt for the lower end of the recommended cooking time. If you don't have an auto-timing switch, which ensures the slow cooker turns to warm when you have reached your specified cooking time, you may want to consider a timing plug, especially if you are out all day and can't monitor your slow cooker.

Contents

Introduction

Slow cooking has been used for as nearly long as we have cooked food, initially as simply an iron pot hung over a fire. It is well known that cowboys would leave their chilli cooking over the dying embers of the fire whilst they went out all day tending their cattle, arriving back hours later to find a delicious hot meal waiting for them. In the home, we have slow cooked for many years with a pot kept on the stove or over the fire for days on end, continually topping up with ingredients.

This whole process of slow cooking was automated in the 1960s with the first electrically powered slow cooker, which was initially produced to cook beans. This innovation was soon discovered to work just as well with other ingredients and the modern-day electric slow cooker was born.

Suits a busy lifestyle

The slow cooker is now enjoying a resurgence in popularity as the advantages it offers over conventional cooking become more compelling. With progressively busier lifestyles, we don't want to spend hours in our kitchens slaving over the stove. More people work part time, full time or work longer hours, with both adults working in most households, thus leaving less time or energy to prepare meals. Many families spend their afternoons after school whizzing children around the locality to various activities, only to return around teatime. The prospect of spending a frantic half hour preparing a meal for hungry children can be daunting and, quite frankly, exhausting. Pre-packaged convenience ready meals may have satisfied this need for some; however, many people are turning their backs on these 'meal solutions', partly due to cost, some due to health reasons and many because they just don't taste that good, and they certainly don't taste home-cooked.

Economical and environmentally friendly

In recent years, our need to reduce our our fuel bills, and our energy consumption generally, has also meant that using a slow cooker now makes both makes economic and ecological sense. The energy consumption of a slow cooker will vary from model to model but it is estimated to be approximately 125–150 watts per hour, compared with a conventional oven which uses approximately 700W per hour. So even though you may use a slow cooker for longer, the overall consumption is still lower, especially if you cook the vegetables in the slow cooker as well! That makes it a really environmentally friendly way of cooking.

The slow cooker is a great cost-saving gadget in another way, too, as it enables us to use cheaper ingredients, again helping to ease the financial burden of life. In particular, the cost of meat is increasing and this is set to continue, especially if we choose to buy free-range or organic produce. The slow, moist cooking process is the perfect way to get tender and succulent results from the tougher cuts of meat that are so much cheaper than chops, steaks or fillets. Other less popular cuts of meat or poultry are also much cheaper to buy. Consider our obsession with the pure, creamy, low-fat chicken breast fillet; their popularity leaves us with an inexpensive, plentiful supply of thighs and drumsticks that are transformed into succulent and tasty morsels when slow cooked.

Hands-off cooking

One of the great things about using a slow cooker is that it is hands-off cooking, whereby you can just leave it to do its thing. It is very tempting to fiddle and interfere but there really is no need and you will extend the slow cooking time by lifting the lid all the time. You really can just leave it, head off to work or out for the day with the kids and not worry about it at all. There is nothing more satisfying than knowing that dinner is prepared. One friend commented that she felt particularly smug on the days when her slow cooker was doing all the work, whilst she went off and got on with other things. Another friend takes her slow cooker on holiday with her to her caravan. Where space is at a premium, the one-pot solution is perfect and she and her family can swan off for the day knowing that dinner will be ready and waiting for them when they return. The Smoky Barbecue Pork Ribs (page 155) and the Texas-style Barbecue Beef (page 181) were of particular interest to her as she thought that they could put these straight on the barbecue when they got back from their day out.

Healthy cooking

When considering the nutritional aspect of slow-cooked food, my view is that overall it is better. The only downside is the loss of some of the more fragile vitamins. The water-soluble vitamins and minerals will leach into the water, which stays with the food and is generally used in the gravy or sauce. If you don't pre-brown the meat in oil, then you will cut down on the fat content of the dish and therefore the calories, although sometimes you will get better results if you pre-brown the meat in order to allow some of the fat to be drained off. This is especially true of higher-fat meats such as lamb. If you are not going to pre-brown, I would always recommend buying lean meats and minces where possible or trimming off any excess fat, as once you start cooking in the slow cooker, the fat has nowhere to go and it is most unappetising to take off the lid only to see a layer of oil on top.

In addition to these direct nutritional advantages, there are indirect ones to slow cooking too. By cooking from scratch, there is less call for fast food or ready meals, and this reduction in processed foods should benefit us nutritionally as home-cooked foods generally have reduced levels of salt and include more fresh and healthy ingredients, such as vegetables.

Vegetarian options

Surprisingly, one area in which slow cooking hasn't quite caught on is with vegetarians. I have a number of friends and colleagues who are vegetarian and they just didn't even think of a slow cooker being for them as they associate it very closely with meat recipes. How wrong they are! Vegetables are fabulous cooked in the slow cooker and, even better, combining pulses and beans is a doddle.

Another advantage presents itself here. If you have one vegetarian in your family, it can sometimes be hard to ensure that you are meeting their needs as you don't just want to give them a plate of vegetables or cook an entirely different meal for them. So using the slow cooker to make up a quantity of a vegetarian meal, such as a Chickpea and Butternut Squash Curry (without the optional chicken, obviously! – see page 44) or a Kerala Sweet Potato and Spinach Curry (page 47), and then freezing them in batches means you can always ensure that you have a meal solution at hand. Plus it's so simple to adapt the recipes, making the Mediterranean Balsamic Vegetables (page 171), for example, taking out a vegetarian portion and then adding some cooked prawns for the non-vegetarians.

Organized around your needs

Taking all these aspects into account, I had a very long think about the way that a slow cooker cookbook should be structured and I fast came to the conclusion that the traditional breakfast, lunch, dinner, dessert chapter approach wasn't really the most useful way of doing this. Going back to the nub of why you buy a slow-cooker in the first place was, in my view, the way forward. I asked many slow cooker owners why they had bought a slow cooker and one word came up repeatedly: time.

Taking this concept in its many forms raised questions that I felt each chapter could answer.

- How much time do you have?
- How long do you need the recipes to cook for?
- When do you use the slow cooker?

Everyone I spoke to about this concept agreed that a time-based approach would make it much easier to find the recipes that met their needs on that particular day. Indeed they felt it would also encourage them to use the slow cooker more, as they could clearly see how the recipes could fit into their lifestyle. So here's how the recipes are organized.

- **All-dayers** Recipes that you know you can put into the slow cooker in the morning and they'll be fine for a good 8–10 hours.

- **The Afternoon Slot** Recipes that take 3–4 hours, are family oriented and enable the slow cooker to be loaded and put on in the afternoon so that the meals are ready for early evening.

- **Chop and Chuck In** It is what it says: recipes where all you need to do is a bit of chopping up and then all the ingredients are chucked in the slow cooker – the ultimate in convenience when you've got about five minutes to prep everything.

- **Just Take Five** If you don't like recipes with extensive ingredients lists, these are for you, as each recipe contains just five main ingredients.

- **Store Cupboard** Here's a batch of recipes for which you should have everything in the cupboard, freezer or veg box, so you can always make a lovely meal.

- **Cheap Eats** Nothing to do with time, but very important when we are all trying to eat well on a reduced budget, this section features cheaper cuts of meat, leftovers or ingredients that are available very cheaply, making these recipes very economical to make.

- **The Weekender** More involved recipes that perhaps require a little more preparation or attention and also recipes, such as stock, that are bases for other recipes.

Each chapter features main courses, vegetarian dishes, soups and desserts as well as other types of recipe, so there should be something to tempt you within each time occasion. Optional ingredients and changes are also given so that the basic recipe can be altered to create a new one and give you the flexibility that you sometimes need or just if you fancy ringing the changes.

Chapter 1

How the Slow Cooker Works

The slow cooker is essentially a heated metal jacket around a ceramic basin. It is the metal jacket that heats up and then this warmth is transferred to the ceramic dish, creating the cooking environment for the food. When the lid is placed on the basin, it seals this environment and so the heat and steam that accumulates stays within the basin retaining all the moisture. It is essential that the lid fits well otherwise this moisture will escape leading to food drying out or worse still burning onto the basin. If there are gaps, I would recommend returning the product to the manufacturer as it will affect the slow-cooking process and lead to ruined recipes. As the moisture seal is so integral it is important that the right amount of liquid is used in the recipes, especially those with the longer cook times. It is not so important for cooking times around the three-hour mark.

Some people insist that all food should be covered with liquid but I have not found this to be essential and so don't be alarmed if a recipe doesn't specify this. What is important is that you do not overfill the slow-cooker basin. Half to three-quarters full is fine. There are often photographs of slow cookers filled to the brim with meat and vegetables – ignore them! The slow cooker will not work efficiently if it is too full and the contents will boil over and burn on the metal jacket.

What do the different heat settings mean?

There is usually more than one setting on a slow cooker and these relate to how quickly the unit heats up to reach a temperature of between 76°C and approx. 138°C. By switching to LOW, the unit will take a couple of hours to get up to temperature, whereas on HIGH this happens within an hour. An AUTO setting is where the slow cooker starts its heating on a HIGH setting for about an hour and then when it reaches temperature, it switches automatically to a LOW setting. Many slow cookers also have a KEEP WARM setting that you can switch to once cooking has finished. The more sophisticated models have automatic timers which allow you to cook on a heat setting for a pre-determined time when it then switches to the KEEP WARM setting.

A word on food safety

As a food scientist and food safety trainer, I am well aware of the food safety risk associated with the poor temperature control of high-risk foods so I was intrigued to test this out for myself. I have taken a number of core temperatures of products in the slow cooker and they are well over the UK temperature requirement of 75°C that ensure that harmful bacteria are killed. I would caution against the use of adding frozen food to the slow cooker, a very popular practice by all accounts. This could potentially cause issues as foods will be in the 'danger zone' for bacterial growth for too long and could, therefore, cause food poisoning. Adding a few frozen vegetables or an ice cube of frozen stock to a dish is not going to cause any issues, but adding large frozen pieces of meat or blocks of frozen ingredients is. This is because the food has to defrost before it can be cooked and this process will take quite a while, resulting in a slow cooker full of food that has been in the 'danger zone' for quite a few hours. You are then totally reliant on the food reaching the all-important 75°C temperature in order to destroy the harmful bacteria but unless you check with a thermometer, this cannot always be guaranteed, especially where you are only cooking for 4–5 hours. If you are going to use frozen ingredients, I would advise that you invest in a thermometer and check out the temperature just to be safe!

What size to buy?

Slow cookers vary in capacity and so it is important to ensure that you have the right size. Base this on the number of mouths that need feeding to ensure no one goes hungry. It is also important to know that the capacity stated is NOT the working capacity as you don't fill up the basin to the top. This will give you a guide.

Number of servings	Total capacity	Usable capacity
6 adults	6–6.5 litres	4.5 litres
4 adults	5 litres	4.0 litres
2 adults/2 children	3.5 litres	2–2.5 litres
2 adults	1.5 litres	1 litre

Basic features available

Basic features for most slow cookers include a removable internal ceramic basin. This makes cleaning much easier and also handy for moving the basin to the preparation area without having to move the entire piece of equipment. This ceramic basin is very susceptible to breaking or cracking if dropped or if subjected to a rapid temperature change. NEVER put the basin in the fridge filled with ingredients and then put straight into the metal heating casing as the temperature change could crack the basin, causing the ingredients to leak into the heated metal casing and burn. A glass lid is standard on most models and is essential to enable us to view the food simmering away and, more importantly, to stop us from succumbing to temptation and lifting the lid. If the glass lid has condensation on it, just give it a tap and the glass will clear, allowing you to see inside.

Additional features available

Additional features available on some models include an internal ceramic bowl that you can also use on the hob or under the grill. This enables you to fry off ingredients in the slow cooker before placing it back in the metal casing to continue cooking. Others are suitable for use in the microwave, although I have to be honest and say that I haven't found that I needed the microwave functionality so far. An indicator light is useful to help identify that the slow cooker is actually on; I have had personal experience of putting the ingredients in the slow cooker, switching the dial onto LOW and going out for the day, only to find on my return that the plug socket wasn't switched on!

There are models with automatic timers that switch off after the required cook time has lapsed. These are particularly useful if you cannot guarantee when you may be back to switch off the appliance, so you just set the timer and you know that the meal won't be ruined. I have even seen a 'buffet style' arrangement of three slow cookers with a capacity of just under 2.5 litres each, a great idea for those of you who entertain or want to make dinner, dessert and maybe an accompaniment as well. Surprisingly, it wasn't that expensive at around £60. More complex slow cookers are available that allow for steaming and frying, which will add flexibility to your cooking. Ranging in price from £15 up to £150, picking the right slow cooker is a tricky decision. The higher end of the market is dominated by digital, programmable models with timers and delays. I would recommend thinking about how you are going to use it first and foremost and then find the model that suits best.

Direct and indirect cooking methods

Most recipes in this book are directly cooked in the slow-cooker basin itself, others use a water bath to cook the food. In order to use the water-bath or bain-marie method, you will need to have a suitably sized container or containers to put inside the basin, so make sure they fit before you fill them with your ingredients. I have used pudding basins or tins and coffee cups in some recipes; ramekins work well too. It's worth looking out for small containers that will fit inside your size of basin. Ceramic, metal and glass work well as do silicone containers.

When direct cooking, some recipes call for the basin to be lined to either prevent sticking or to aid removal of the cooked food. Foil, parchment or greaseproof paper is suitable for this. For a longer-term solution and a time saver, buy a sheet of the re-usable non-stock liner and cut it to size for the base of your slow cooker. If you are feeling very skilful, include long straps in the cut-out shape to assist with lifting out the liner, or just place a long greaseproof strap under the liner. There are also specially shaped liners that fit over the entire basin. These can be purchased online as they appear to only be available in the USA at the moment. They can be quite expensive though as most are not re-usable.

Adapting conventional recipes

If you want to adapt a conventional recipe for use in the slow cooker, bear in mind that you will not need as much liquid because very little is lost during the slow-cooking process. I would start by reducing the liquid by half and seeing how the dish turns out. You may want to choose a time to do this when you are around just in case it is not sufficient. Recipes that normally take from 30 minutes to an hour will take 4–6 hours on a LOW setting or 3–4 hours for a HIGH setting. For recipes that take an hour or longer, they will take 8–10 hours on LOW and 6–8 on HIGH.

Looking after your slow cooker

Always read your slow cooker manual carefully as models do vary quite a lot in terms of whether or not they are dishwasher proof. Most have a dishwasher-proof basin, but some state that the lid should be washed by hand. I always recommend putting hot soapy water into the basin after you've used the slow-cooker basin so that you can start to dissolve off any remnants of your meal immediately, then pop in the dishwasher just before you start it. NEVER immerse the metal heating unit in water as it is an electrical item and this will damage it. Unplug and use a damp sponge or cloth with diluted detergent and wipe down thoroughly. Many advise using vinegar or a non-abrasive cleaner to remove any water spots and stains.

Chapter 2

Ingredients

It's not just about stew! The slow cooker is great for long, moist cooking as we know but this should not restrict it to stew or curry, even if these are delicious from the slow cooker. The slow-cooking method is perfect for cuts of meat such as pork ribs, beef brisket or shoulder of lamb whereby the meat becomes soft, juicy and succulent. Vegetables such as peppers and mushrooms are fantastic in the slow cooker as they concentrate down and become intense, fabulous versions of their fresh selves.

Establishing a good store cupboard

As you get to know the recipes and become more familiar with the ingredients, you'll start to establish your own list of essentials and keep your store cupboard replenished so that you can have all the ingredients to hand to make your favourite recipes. A well-stocked cupboard is essential so that you have ingredients to hand and just have to shop for the main fresh components.

As a minimum, I would recommend having:
- Salt
- Pepper (freshly ground black pepper preferably)
- Garlic
- Chilli powder
- Italian mixed dried herbs
- Ground cumin
- Ground coriander
- Ground ginger
- Bay leaves
- A variety of stock cubes or stock pots or concentrates
- Worcestershire sauce
- Soy sauce
- Tomato purée
- Tins of chopped tomatocs
- Passata
- Plain flour

These items are also good to have:
- Dried oregano
- Rosemary

- Smoked paprika
- Chinese five-spice powder
- Red wine vinegar
- White wine vinegar
- Frozen vegetables

I also make sure I've got some basic fresh ingredients that I can use in many of the recipes; these include onions, root vegetables such as carrots and parsnips, courgettes and peppers. These will last a good few weeks if stored in the vegetable box in your fridge. Other vegetables that work really well are mushrooms, sweet potato, butternut squash, aubergine and sweetcorn. Green vegetables are generally not great slow cooked as they can go very mushy. Also, leafy green vegetables such as broccoli and cabbage can start to smell sulphurous as some of the compounds break down during the slow-cooking process. If you want to add these to your dishes, I would cook them separately and add at the end of cooking. Potatoes are exceptionally good in the slow cooker and hold their shape well. Use waxy potatoes or new potatoes as these are particularly resilient to extended cooking times. It is strange but true that root vegetables and potatoes take longer to cook in the slow cooker than the meat and therefore it is worth remembering to put these on the bottom of the basin with the meat on top.

Most fruit works very well; exceptions are those that brown, such as apples and pears, but the trick here is to cut them up and put them straight into the slow cooker and mix with the other ingredients, sprinkle with a little lemon juice to slow the browning process. If there is a time gap, chop them into cold water, which will also slow the browning process.

Cooking meat, fish, poultry and game

As mentioned in the Introduction, it is the cheaper cuts of meat that do well in a slow cooker. You can in fact use more expensive cuts but these do tend to dry out and go a bit leathery or fibrous. The best meat cuts for slow cooking are those which have done the most work during the animal's life, such as neck, shoulder, shin or rump. As a general rule, the nearer the hoof or the horn, the tougher the meat. Chuck steaks, silverside, topside or shank are sometime sold as named cuts of meat. Even though they are cheap, I would avoid using the very fatty cuts such as breast or belly as these will just render down to a very greasy, fatty meat in the slow cooker and will not be pleasant. It is a false economy to buy cheaper, fattier meat if you are going to throw away a large proportion of the fat. The same thing goes for minced beef and lamb: the cheaper products are higher in fat so try to buy products with less than 12 per cent fat, otherwise I would recommend frying these off prior to putting in the slow cooker.

Fish is a much more delicate ingredient to work with and the slow-cooking process can be disastrous for the more fragile types of fish. The recipes in this book tend to use more robust types of fish such as salmon, tuna and monkfish as their meatier texture holds up well to a good few hours of cooking. A few recipes have included the cooking technique known as 'en papillote', whereby the fish is cooked in a sealed parcel made of foil or parchment, sealing all the flavours in and protecting the fish from falling apart. The slow cooker can be used as a steamer in this way too for all types of fish.

Poultry and game are very good in the slow cooker as they hold up well to the slow-cooking process. Cheaper cuts of chicken such as thighs and legs are particularly tasty as the meat does just slip off the bone. Game cooks beautifully well especially when in a rich sauce or red wine to really bring out the best flavour of the meat. Surprisingly successful is roasting a whole chicken, whilst I know you are not technically roasting it, the slow-cooking process ensures that the breast meat does not dry out and if you have the oven on to cook your roast potatoes, it does only take 15 minutes for the slow-cooked chicken to brown off. Always remember to line the basin with some foil or parchment to lift the chicken out, if you use a meat fork to lift it out all the meat will fall off the carcass!

Cooking pulses and beans

Pulses and beans are exceptionally nutritious and an excellent source of non-meat protein, they also count towards your fruit and vegetable intake so we really should be eating more. The slow-cooking process is perfect for these ingredients and they are consequently to be found in many of the recipes in the book. It is important to remember that certain dried pulses and beans need to be soaked in water overnight and then boiled vigorously in water for at least 10 minutes. This is essential to remove certain compounds naturally present that can be toxic. Always refer to the cooking instructions for guidance on safely preparing these ingredients. Lentils are a pulse that does not need boiling, so these can just be added to the slow-cooker basin, while tinned pulses and beans do not need soaking either as these have already been heat treated.

Cooking rice and pasta

I always recommend using easy-cook rice varieties as these have been par-boiled, which helps to wash out the excess starch. The result is that the grains become less sticky and mushy and so are a better option when slow cooking. Pasta can become very soggy when slow cooked so the recipes where pasta features tend to be cooked for only a couple of hours.

Using dairy products

Dairy products and long cooking times do not mix well as the products split and ruin the dish. Always stir in creams, milk or crème fraîche at the end of cooking to stop this from happening. Making a roux sauce for dishes such as the macaroni cheese or lasagne is fine as the addition of the flour stabilizes the sauce and it does not split.

Using herbs and spices

Most herbs and spices are brilliant in the slow cooker, the slow-cooking process serving to marinate the ingredients in the various spice blends, herbs and rubs that feature in these recipes. Because the cooking is in a sealed environment, there is far less liquid lost and so the flavours will concentrate and develop over time; this is especially important when using dried herbs as the flavours will strengthen considerably during the cooking process and if too much is used they can become bitter tasting. Fresh, leafy green herbs such as basil and coriander are best added at the end of cooking otherwise they lose their lovely fragrant flavours. The fabulous range of spice pastes available nowadays is such a boon for cooks who don't want to use jars of sauces. They are, in my view, fantastic quality and produce excellent results. Jerk, rendang, teriyaki, Thai and Moroccan styles are just a few of the massive ranges available. It may seem quite expensive for a small jar, but it is much cheaper than buying all the ingredients to make up the paste yourself. There are a few recipes with spice paste ingredients in this book if you want to make up your own paste and freeze it. Otherwise, use a bought spice paste – you won't be disappointed.

Which liquids, stocks and gravies to use

For convenience, stock cubes and liquids are very good and the quality is improving all the time. For best results, always add hot stock to the basin as this gives the heating up a head start. Alternatively if you want to slow things down a bit, add warm stock. To make a thicker sauce or gravy, I always roll the main ingredients, such as meat or mushrooms, in seasoned flour. Any flour will do and season with salt and freshly ground black pepper. Wheat flour is the best to use as the starch gelatinizes at between 52°C–54°C whereas maize or cornstarch gelatinizes at a far higher temperature so is less likely to thicken effectively in a slow cooker. If you have time, have a go at the recipes to make your own stock from a chicken carcass, beef bones (see page 190-3). These can then be used either the next day or frozen into small containers for use at another time.

Getting the best out of your slow cooker

1. Buy a slow cooker with the correct capacity for your family size (see page 14).
2. Make sure the lid of your slow cooker fits tightly.
3. Don't overfill your slow cooker.
4. Resist the temptation to take off the lid while cooking unless instructed to do so.
5. Never put your slow-cooker basin in the fridge and then into the metal heating jacket.
6. Always defrost meat and fish or large blocks of vegetables.
7. Put root vegetables and potatoes at the bottom of the slow-cooker basin.
8. Avoid very fatty cuts of meat and remove as much visible fat as possible.
9. Don't use creams or milk in longer-cooking recipes
10. Add green vegetables, dairy products and soft green herbs at the end of cooking.

Conversion charts

This book provides metric measurements, but those who prefer imperial, or who want to use US measures can use these conversions (see opposite).

Weights

Metric	Imperial	US cups
25g	1oz	
50g	2oz	
75g	3oz	
100g	4oz	1 cup flour etc.
150g	5oz	
175g	6oz	1 cup sultanas etc.
200g	7oz	
225g	8oz	1 cup butter, sugar, etc.
250g	9oz	
300g	10oz	
350g	12oz	
400g	14oz	
450g	16oz	

Temperatures

Metric	Imperial	Gas
110°C	225°F	$1/4$
120°C	250°F	$1/2$
140°C	275°F	1
150°C	300°F	2
160°C	325°F	3
180°C	350°F	4
190°C	375°F	5
200°C	400°F	6
220°C	425°F	7
230°C	450°F	8
240°C	475°F	9

Liquids

Metric	Imperial	US cups
5ml	1 tsp	1 tsp
15ml	1 tbsp	1 tbsp
50ml	2fl oz	3 tbsp
60ml	2$1/2$ fl oz	$1/4$ cup
75ml	3fl oz	$1/3$ cup
100ml	4fl oz	scant $1/2$ cup
125ml	4$1/2$ fl oz	$1/2$ cup
150ml	5fl oz	$2/3$ cup
200ml	7fl oz	scant 1 cup
250ml	10fl oz	1 cup
300ml	$1/2$pt	1$1/4$ cups
350ml	12fl oz	1$1/3$ cups
450ml	$3/4$pt	1$3/4$ cups
500ml	20fl oz	2 cups
600ml	1pt	2$1/2$ cups

Measurements

Metric	Imperial
5cm	2in
10cm	4in
13cm	5in
15cm	6in
18cm	7in
20cm	8in
25cm	10in
30cm	12in

Chapter 3
All-dayers

This chapter is packed with recipes that you know you can put into the slow cooker in the morning and they'll be fine for a good 8–10 hours – perfect for you to come home to after a long day at work.

Broths seem to have gone out of fashion, as has pearl barley, but I think they should make a comeback. This hearty soup is a perfect winter warmer and needs no further accompaniments. Another option is to use stewing beef and beef stock instead of the lamb.

Lamb and Barley Broth

Serves 4

300–400g lamb (any cut will do), trimmed of any visible fat and cut into bite-sized pieces

1/2 onion, chopped

1 large carrot, peeled and chopped

1 turnip or parsnip, peeled and chopped

1 celery stick, chopped

125g new potatoes, peeled and cut into bite-sized chunks

1 garlic clove, crushed

1/2 tsp dried mixed herbs

1 bay leaf

60g pearl barley

1.5 litres hot lamb stock

Salt and freshly ground black pepper

1   Put the lamb into the slow-cooker basin and add the chopped vegetables, crushed garlic, mixed herbs and bay leaf.

2   Rinse the pearl barley in cold water, drain and place on top of the vegetables. Pour over the hot stock.

3   Place the lid on securely and cook on HIGH for 3–4 hours or LOW for 6–8 hours until the meat is tender.

4   When cooked, season to taste with salt and pepper.

Slow cooking the chicken pieces in the rich Spanish flavours of smoked paprika and chorizo infuses the meat with fabulous intensity and ensures the meat stays moist.

Spanish Chicken and Chorizo

Serves 4

1   Mix together the dry rub ingredients and roll the chicken in the mixture to coat.

2   Rub the garlic cloves around the slow-cooker basin, then crush them and add them to the basin with the chopped onion.

3   Place the chicken and chorizo on top of the onion and garlic, then add the olives and the herbs.

4   Mix the hot chicken stock and the wine, then stir in the chopped tomatoes. Pour into the basin and mix thoroughly. Add the butter beans, if using, and stir again.

5   Put the lid on securely and cook on a LOW setting for 8–10 hours until the chicken is meltingly tender, adding the prawns, if using, for the last hour of cooking. Serve with boiled rice or potatoes.

For the dry rub
1 tsp smoked paprika
1 tsp salt
1 tsp freshly ground
   black pepper
1 tbsp plain flour

For the chicken
4 chicken legs, cut into
   4 thighs and 4
   drumsticks
2 garlic cloves, cut in
   half
1 onion, chopped
150g chorizo, chopped
75g pitted black olives
Fresh bouquet garni of
   sprigs of fresh
   rosemary, sage and
   bay
300ml hot chicken
   stock
150ml red wine
400g tin of chopped
   tomatoes
400g tin of butter
   beans (optional)
225g frozen prawns
   (optional)
Boiled rice or potatoes,
   to serve

This is a whole chicken dish that will cook slowly over the day, ready for popping into a hot oven if you want to brown it off. You can cook a bigger chicken, just make sure it will fit in your slow cooker first!

Lemon and Garlic Chicken

Serves 4

1.25–1.5kg chicken
1 onion, chopped
1 carrot, peeled and
    chopped
1 garlic clove, sliced
½ lemon, sliced
3 lemon thyme sprigs
300ml hot chicken
    stock
Salt and freshly ground
    black pepper

1   Place a layer of foil inside the slow-cooker basin, put the chicken on top and surround with the chopped onion and carrot.

2   Lay the slices of garlic and lemon over the top of the chicken and top with the lemon thyme sprigs.

3   Pour the hot chicken stock over the top and season with salt and pepper.

4   Put the lid on tightly and cook on LOW for 8–10 hours until the chicken is cooked through. Always check by putting a knife into the thickest part of the thigh. The juices should run clear, not pink.

5   Alternatively, for a quicker cooking time, cook on HIGH for 4–5 hours, again checking that the juices run clear.

6   Remember to lift out using the foil otherwise the chicken will fall to pieces.

Everyone loves a sweet and sour chicken and using the slow cooker for this dish is so straightforward. There really is nothing like using the fresh ingredients, but it's not a problem if you want to make life even easier and use a jar of sweet and sour sauce, although the pineapple will lose its flavour, so I add a few chunks of chopped pineapple at the end.

Sweet and Sour Chicken

Serves 4

1   Drain the pineapple, reserving the juice. Chop 2 slices of the pineapple and reserve.

2   Put the sliced vegetables, crushed garlic and grated ginger in the slow-cooker basin.

3   Add the pineapple juice, sugar, tomato purée, wine vinegar, soy sauce and hot chicken stock and stir well.

4   Season the flour with salt and pepper, then toss the sliced chicken breast in the flour. Add it to the basin and stir in.

5   Put the lid on tightly and cook on LOW for 8–10 hours until the chicken and vegetables are tender.

6   Add the reserved pineapple chunks, stir through and serve with noodles or rice, garnished with sesame seeds and sliced spring onions.

400g tin of pineapple rings in juice
1 carrot, peeled and thinly sliced into strips
1 red pepper, deseeded and sliced into strips
1 onion, thinly sliced into rings
1 garlic clove, crushed
2cm piece of fresh or frozen root ginger, grated
2 tbsp soft dark brown sugar
1 tbsp tomato purée
50ml red wine vinegar
1 tbsp dark soy sauce
200ml hot chicken stock
1 tbsp plain flour
Salt and freshly ground black pepper
500g chicken breast, sliced into strips
Noodles or rice, to serve
Sliced spring onions and sesame seeds to garnish

A slow-cooker classic for sure, this dish yields spectacular results every time with very little effort.

Beef Bourguignon

Serves 4

1 garlic clove, cut in half
200g small shallots, peeled and left whole
200g small button mushrooms, lightly washed
30g plain flour
Salt and freshly ground black pepper
900g–1kg casserole steak, cut into chunks
100g smoked back bacon rashers, rinded and cut into pieces
150ml hot beef stock
250ml red wine
1 tsp sugar
Bouquet garni of bay leaf, rosemary and thyme
Mashed potatoes or rice, to serve

1   Rub the garlic clove around the slow-cooker basin, then chop or crush and add it to the basin.

2   Add the shallots and mushrooms.

3   Season the flour with salt and pepper and place in a shallow bowl. Coat the beef and bacon in the seasoned flour, then add them to the basin.

4   Mix the hot beef stock, wine and sugar and stir to dissolve. Pour onto the meat and vegetables and add the bouquet garni.

5   Cover tightly with a lid and cook on a LOW setting for 8–10 hours until the meat is tender and the sauce is rich.

6   Discard the bouquet garni and serve with mashed potatoes or rice.

A classic Belgian dish that uses dark Belgian beer to give the beef an extra flavour boost, along with mustard bread that cooks down to give the gravy a lovely thick texture.

Beef Carbonnade

Serves 4

1 Season the flour with salt and pepper. Roll the beef in the seasoned flour and place in the slow-cooker basin.

2 Add the chopped onion, potatoes, carrot and bacon to the basin.

3 Add the beer to the hot beef stock and pour over the meat and vegetables. Add the bay leaf and crushed garlic.

4 Spread the mustard onto the slices of bread and cut each slice into 4 triangles. Arrange the bread in a layer over the ingredients, mustard-side down.

5 Put the lid on tightly and cook on LOW for 8–10 hours until the beef is tender and the bread has melted into the casserole.

6 Serve with mashed potatoes or boiled rice.

1 tbsp plain flour
Salt and freshly ground
    black pepper
800g stewing beef, cut
    into chunks
1 large onion, chopped
250g waxy potatoes,
    peeled and chopped
1 large carrot, peeled
    and chopped
4 back bacon rashers,
    rinded and cut into
    small pieces
400ml dark beer,
    preferably Belgian
300ml hot beef stock
1 bay leaf
1 garlic clove, crushed
2 tbsp wholegrain
    mustard
4 slices of bread, crusts
    removed
Mashed potatoes or
    boiled rice, to serve

This is such a simple way of cooking a ham joint. It saves a fortune in buying pre-packed sliced ham and can be sliced thickly and used in other dishes or served as a gammon slice with pineapple.

Easy-peasy Boiled Ham

Serves 4

750g–1.5kg bacon or
   gammon joint
10 black peppercorns
4 cloves
1 bay leaf
1 tbsp golden syrup
750ml boiling water
250ml apple juice

1   Lay a piece of kitchen foil in the base of the slow-cooker basin to help with lifting out the ham at the end of cooking. Place the gammon in the basin and add the spices.

2   Mix the syrup with the boiling water and apple juice, then pour over the gammon.

3   Place the lid on tightly and cook on LOW for 8–10 hours or cook on HIGH for 5-6 hours. The gammon will be beautifully tender. Lift it out of the slow cooker using the foil and drain before slicing.

4   Serve hot or cold.

Slow cooking a lamb curry is a sure-fire way to bring out the best in all the ingredients. Succulent lamb and the rich fragrant tomato sauce is characteristic of a lamb Rogan Josh.

Lamb Rogan Josh
Serves 4

1   Grease the slow-cooker basin with a little oil and turn the slow cooker to HIGH. Add the crushed garlic, the cardamom, cloves and coriander seeds to the basin.

2   Mix the rest of the spices into the flour, then add to the basin and mix everything together.

3   Add the lamb to the basin and coat well with the flour and spice mix.

4   Stir in the chopped onion and chopped tomatoes and mix well.

5   Put the lid on tightly and cook on LOW for 8–10 hours.

6   When ready to serve, stir through a little knob of butter to give the curry a nice glossy finish, sprinkle on the fresh coriander and serve with the rice or naan bread and a spoonful of crème fraîche on the side.

A little oil, for greasing
3 garlic cloves, crushed
3 cardamom pods
3 cloves
$1/2$ tsp coriander seeds
1 tsp ground ginger
$1/2$ tsp ground cinnamon
1 tsp ground cumin
2 tsp paprika
1 tsp cayenne pepper
1 tbsp plain flour
500–600g lamb, trimmed of any visible fat and cut into 2–3cm chunks
1 onion, finely chopped
400g tin of chopped tomatoes
A knob of butter
A handful of fresh coriander, chopped
1 heaped tbsp crème fraîche
Boiled rice and naan bread, to serve

Make up the paste and marinate the lamb overnight in a container in the fridge. Once cooked, the tagine flavours will mature fabulously so this always tastes better on day two or three – if, of course, there is any left! If you don't have time to make up the paste, you can use a jar of ready-made tagine paste.

Lamb Tagine
Serves 4

For the tagine paste
1 tbsp tomato purée
1 tbsp clear honey
1 tbsp lemon juice
1 garlic clove, crushed
1 tsp ground ginger
1 tsp ground cumin
1 tsp ground coriander
2 tsp paprika
1/2 tsp cayenne pepper

For the tagine
600g stewing lamb, trimmed of any fat and diced
1 small onion, finely chopped
1 red pepper, deseeded and sliced
100g ready-to-eat dried apricots or prunes
400g tin of chickpeas, drained and rinsed
450ml hot lamb stock
400g tin of cherry tomatoes
Flatbreads and couscous, to serve

1 In a small bowl, combine all the ingredients for the tagine paste until you have a thick paste.

2 If marinating overnight, place the lamb and the paste in a bowl (not the slow-cooker basin) and coat the lamb well. Palace in the fridge overnight. If cooking immediately, put the lamb pieces in the slow-cooker basin and add the paste, mixing well to coat the lamb pieces.

3 Add the chopped onion and sliced red pepper to the basin along with the apricots and chickpeas.

4 Pour over the hot lamb stock and the tomatoes and stir well.

5 Place the lid on the cooker and cook on LOW for 8–10 hours until the meat is tender and the sauce fragrant.

6 Serve with flatbreads or couscous for a great Moroccan-inspired meal.

NOTE
Never put your slow-cooker basin straight into the slow cooker if you have left it in the fridge overnight. The temperature change will potentially crack it. Always store the food in a different container.

The flavour of the mushroom is celebrated in this dish as they concentrate and intensify during slow cooking and the stock thickens beautifully to give a glossy, rich finish. This can also be used as a vegetarian alternative to a meaty pie filling (see page 186).

Mushroom Ragout

Serves 4

1 Rub the garlic halves around the inside of the slow-cooker basin, then chop the garlic finely and add it to the basin with the chopped onion.

2 Pour the hot vegetable stock over the dried mushrooms and leave to rehydrate for a few minutes. Stir in the soy sauce.

3 Mix together the smoked paprika, pepper and flour. Add the mushrooms and coat with the seasoned flour, then add to the slow-cooker basin.

4 Pour the stock liquid and porcini mushrooms into the slow-cooker basin and mix well. Don't worry if the flour goes lumpy.

5 Place the lid on the slow cooker and cook on LOW for 6–8 hours until the sauce is thick and glossy.

6 Serve with boiled rice or mashed potatoes.

1 garlic clove, cut in half
1 small onion, finely chopped
600ml hot vegetable stock
20g dried porcini mushrooms
1 tbsp soy sauce
1 tsp smoked paprika
1/2 tsp freshly ground black pepper
2 tbsp plain flour
200–300g chestnut mushrooms, chopped into even-sized pieces
125g shiitake mushrooms, chopped into even-sized pieces
Boiled rice or mashed potatoes, to serve

This is a great dish to make up and then freeze in portions as it makes a lovely vegetable accompaniment to other curries.

Chickpea and Butternut Squash Curry
Serves 4 as a main course or 6 as an accompaniment

For the spice mix
1 tsp ground cumin
1 tsp chilli powder
1 tsp salt
2 tsp garam masala

For the curry
2 large garlic cloves,
    cut in half
2 large onions, finely
    chopped
400g butternut squash,
    skinned and cut into
    2cm cubes
3 x 400g tins of
    chickpeas, rinsed and
    drained
200g frozen spinach,
    defrosted and
    drained (optional)
1 vegetable stock cube
3 x 400g tins of
    chopped tomatoes
55g butter
Rice or naan bread, to
    serve

1   Mix together all the ingredients for the spice mix.

2   Rub the garlic halves around the inside of the slow-cooker basin, then chop the garlic finely and add it to the basin along with the chopped onions and the spices and mix together well.

3   Add the butternut squash to the basin and mix with the spices.

4   Add the drained chickpeas and the spinach, if using, and mix well again. Sprinkle over the stock cube. Add the chopped tomatoes and stir well.

5   Place the lid on the slow cooker and cook on HIGH for 8–10 hours until the butternut squash is softened.

6   When ready to serve, add the butter and stir well. Serve with rice or naan bread.

OPTION
Just use 2 tins of chickpeas and add 250g chicken, cut into bite-sized chunks, with the squash.

Vegetarian dishes feature heavily in Kerala cuisine and as coconut grows in great numbers in the region they are included in many of the recipes. Tamarind paste is now widely available and gives an unusual sour, fruity flavour to dishes.

Kerala Sweet Potato and Spinach Curry

Serves 4

1 Put the diced sweet potato, the spinach and sliced onion in the slow-cooker basin.

2 Mix the chopped chillies with the grated ginger, crushed garlic, dry spices and tamarind paste.

3 Pour the coconut milk into a jug, add the boiling water and mix in the spice paste until blended. Pour over the sweet potato and spinach.

4 Put the lid on tightly and cook on LOW for 8–9 hours until the sweet potato has softened.

5 Serve with boiled rice or naan bread.

OPTION
Add 220g cooked king prawns for the last half an hour of cooking.

500g sweet potato, peeled and chopped into 2cm cubes
200g frozen spinach, defrosted and drained
1 onion, sliced
1 red chilli, deseeded and chopped
1 green chilli, deseeded and chopped
1 tbsp freshly grated root ginger
2 garlic cloves, crushed
1 tsp ground coriander
1 tsp ground cumin
1/2 tsp ground turmeric
1 tbsp tamarind paste
400g tin of coconut milk
200ml boiling water
Boiled rice or naan bread, to serve

The long cooking time really gives the fruit the chance to condense down to a thick, intensely flavoured compote. As an alternative to serving warm with ice cream, you can serve with extra thick yoghurt, put a spoonful on top of porridge, or use it as a fresh fruit spread on your toast.

Vanilla Autumn Fruit Compote

Serves 4

200–300g (4–6) plums, stoned and quartered
350g (3–4) nectarines, stoned and cut into 8 pieces
350g (3–4) peaches, stoned and cut into 8 pieces
2 tsp vanilla extract
2 tbsp caster sugar
100ml orange juice
Ice cream, to serve

1   Prepare the fruit, making sure the pieces are roughly even-sized. Place in the slow-cooker basin.

2   Add the vanilla extract, sugar and orange juice and stir well.

3   Put the lid on tightly and cook on a LOW setting for 8–9 hours.

4   Remove the lid and continue to cook on LOW for another 30 minutes to allow the compote to reduce and thicken up.

5   Serve warm with ice cream.

OPTION
Add 2 tbsp marsala at the end if you wish to booze it up.

A truly classic dessert, the rich port seeps into the pears and the spicing is subtle but delicious. Choose vanilla for a creamy flavour or cinnamon for a more spicy result.

Port-poached Pears

Serves 4

1 Peel the pears, leaving the stalk on. Place in the slow-cooker basin on their sides.

2 Dissolve the sugar in the port and pour over the pears.

3 Add the spices and top up with boiling water until the pears are covered.

4 Put the lid on tightly and cook on LOW for 8–10 hours until the pears are tender.

5 Serve with vanilla custard or ice cream.

4–6 pears
100g soft dark brown sugar
150ml port
2 whole star anise
1 cinnamon stick or vanilla pod
Vanilla custard or ice cream, to serve

Chapter

4

The Afternoon Slot

All the recipes in this chapter take three to four hours to cook. They are family oriented and enable the slow cooker to be loaded and put on in the afternoon, perhaps before setting off to pick up the kids from school.

Add extra chilli if you like your food extra spicy and add the noodles right at the end to make this delicious and filling soup.

Spicy Chicken Noodle Broth
Serves 4 as a starter or 2 for supper

1 litre hot chicken stock
1 tbsp dark soy sauce
1 tsp Thai fish sauce
1 tbsp vegetable oil
2 chicken breasts, chopped into bite-sized chunks
1 red chilli, deseeded and chopped
1 garlic clove, crushed
200g pack of stir-fry oriental vegetables
150g pack of pre-cooked udon noodles

1 Pour the hot chicken stock, soy sauce and fish sauce into the slow-cooker basin.

2 Heat the oil in a frying pan. Add the chicken and brown for a few minutes, then add the chopped chilli and crushed garlic.

3 Add the vegetables and mix into the rest of the ingredients in the slow-cooker basin.

4 Put the lid on tightly and cook on LOW for 3 hours.

5 When cooked, add the noodles and stir through. Cover again and leave on LOW for 5 minutes to warm through before serving.

A rich Spanish-style soup with fabulous large butter beans or judia beans. These beans are a staple of Spanish cooking and go so well with a tomato-based soup. The pepper cooks down to a lovely sweetness and the chorizo adds that savoury kick. For extra heat, use a spicy chorizo sausage.

Sweet Pepper, Chorizo and Butter Bean Soup

Serves 4

1 Put the chopped onion and crushed garlic into the slow-cooker basin. Add the chopped chorizo and peppers.

2 Sprinkle over the paprika, then pour in the hot vegetable stock and the passata. Add the butter beans and stir well.

3 Place the lid on tightly and cook on HIGH for 3–4 hours.

4 When cooking time has finished, season to taste with salt and pepper.

1 onion, chopped
1 garlic clove, crushed
150g chorizo sausage, chopped
200g red or yellow peppers, deseeded and chopped
2 tsp smoked paprika
900ml hot vegetable stock
300ml tomato passata
235g tin of butter beans, drained and rinsed
Salt and freshly ground black pepper

This Indian-style rice and fish dish is a perfect supper dish for all the family. It is, of course, traditionally served at breakfast so you could make this the night before and warm some up for a breakfast treat.

Kedgeree
Serves 4

300g smoked haddock, skinned and chopped into large chunks
1 onion, finely diced
1 garlic clove, crushed
300ml hot fish stock
300ml milk
1 tsp medium curry powder
$1/2$ tsp cumin
250g easy-cook long-grain or basmati rice

To serve
1 tbsp crème fraîche
1 tbsp chopped fresh parsley or coriander
2 hard-boiled eggs, quartered

1 Put the chunks of smoked mackerel into the slow-cooker basin and add the diced onion and crushed garlic.

2 Mix together the hot fish stock, milk, curry powder and cumin and pour over the fish.

3 Add the rice and stir well.

4 Place the lid on the basin and cook on LOW for 4–5 hours until the rice has absorbed all the liquid.

5 Stir in the crème fraîche, sprinkle with the chopped parsley or coriander and serve garnished with the hard-boiled eggs.

This is a very quick to prepare – a family favourite that will become second nature to cook. You can leave it for longer, if required, and the flavour will only improve. I use the same basic recipe ingredients to make an all-in-one Lasagne (see page 62).

Bolognese Sauce

Serves 4

1   Preheat the slow cooker on high and grease the basin with the vegetable oil. Rub the garlic clove around the basin, then chop and add to the basin.

2   Add the chopped onion, pepper, courgette and mushrooms.

3   Add the beef mince and stir the ingredients together.

4   Sprinkle over the stock cube and herbs. Add the tomato pasta sauce and the chopped tomatoes and mix really well.

5   Put the lid on tightly and cook on HIGH for 3–4 hours until rich and tasty.

6   Serve with pasta.

1 tsp vegetable oil
1 garlic clove, cut in half
1 small onion, finely chopped
$\frac{1}{2}$ red pepper, finely chopped
$\frac{1}{2}$ courgette, finely chopped
4 mushrooms, finely chopped
400–450g lean beef mince
1 beef stock cube
1 tsp dried oregano
200g jar of tomato pasta sauce
400g tin of chopped tomatoes
Freshly boiled pasta, to serve

No one expects they would be able to cook a lasagne in a slow cooker so this is a surprise boon for all. No pre-cooking of the meat or the pasta is required so it is much easier than the conventional method – especially if you use a jar of white sauce from the cupboard.

Lasagne
Serves 4

For the meat sauce
Ingredients as listed for
   Bolognese Sauce
   (page 61)

For the lasagne
6–8 lasagne sheets

For the white sauce
25g butter
25g plain flour
250ml milk
1/2 tsp English mustard
Salt and freshly ground
   black pepper
110g Cheddar cheese

1   In a separate bowl, mix all the ingredients for the Bolognese sauce, following steps 1 to 4 of the recipe on page 61.

2   To make your own white sauce, melt the butter in a pan and stir in the flour. Cook over a low heat for 1 minute, stirring. Take off the heat and beat in the milk a little at a time until everything is well mixed and smooth. Season with the mustard, salt and black pepper. Return to the heat and bring to the boil, add half the cheese and stir in.

3   In the slow-cooker basin, layer up the meat sauce and the pasta sheets, ensuring that you have at least 3 layers of pasta to absorb the liquid.

4   Finish with a layer of meat, followed by a layer of the white sauce.

5   Put the lid on tightly and cook on a HIGH setting for 5–6 hours until bubbling.

6   When cooked, sprinkle the rest of the cheese on the top to serve. If your slow-cooker basin is flameproof, place under a hot grill for a bubbling cheesy top.

Lamb is one ingredient that really does benefit from frying off before you put it in the slow cooker, as doing so removes that excess fat that can ruin a slow-cooked dish. If you prefer, use aubergine instead of courgette – both are authentic ingredients in typical Greek moussaka.

Lamb, Courgette and Potato Moussaka

Serves 4

1. Heat a frying pan and fry off the lamb with the chopped onion, crushed garlic and the allspice until browned.

2. Pour off the excess fat, then stir in the tomatoes and oregano.

3. Arrange the potato slices on the bottom of the slow-cooker basin and layer the slices round the edges. Season well with salt and pepper, then top with one-third of the lamb mix.

4. Arrange the courgettes on top of the mince layer, and season well with salt and pepper. Spoon the rest of the lamb mix on top of the courgettes.

5. Make the white sauce by melting the butter in a small pan, then stirring in the flour. Mix well and cook over a low heat until it boils, stirring continuously. Remove from the heat and gradually whisk in the milk a little at a time, whisking all the time. When all the milk has been added, bring back to the boil and keep whisking until the sauce has thickened. Pour the sauce evenly over the top of the lamb layer.

6. Place the lid on tightly and cook on HIGH for 3–4 hours until bubbling.

7. When cooked, sprinkle the grated cheese on top and serve with a fresh green salad.

400g lean lamb mince
1 onion, finely chopped
2 garlic cloves, crushed
$1/2$ tsp allspice
400g tin of chopped
    tomatoes
$1/2$ tsp dried oregano
2 large potatoes,
    peeled and thinly
    sliced
Salt and freshly ground
    black pepper
2 courgettes, sliced
    lengthways

For the sauce
15g butter
1 tbsp plain flour
200ml milk
25g cheese, grated
Fresh green salad, to
    serve

This is a quick and easy but fragrant curry that only takes a few hours in the slow cooker.

Thai Green Chicken Curry

Serves 4

400ml reduced-fat coconut milk

200g green Thai curry paste

1 red pepper, deseeded and sliced

1 onion, sliced

250–300g chicken breast, cut into bite-sized chunks

2 tbsp chopped fresh coriander

1 lime

Thai fragrant rice, to serve

1   Mix together the coconut milk and Thai paste in the slow-cooker basin, then add the sliced pepper and onion and the chopped chicken.

2   Put the lid on tightly and cook on HIGH for 3 hours until the chicken is beautifully tender.

3   When ready to serve, stir through half the coriander and squeeze the juice of the lime over the top. Garnish with the remaining coriander and serve with Thai fragrant rice.

OPTION
Substitute the chicken with 250g cooked prawns.

An easy and timeless classic for the family to enjoy, you can make your own white sauce or use a jar when you are really short of time. Keep one in the cupboard just in case you need a store cupboard version.

Macaroni Cheese

Serves 4

1 To make the white sauce, melt the butter in a pan, stir in the flour and cook over a low heat for a minute, stirring continuously.

2 Take off the heat and beat in the milk and water a little at a time until it is all mixed well and smooth. Season with the mustard, salt and black pepper. Return to the heat and bring to the boil, stirring continuously. Add to the slow-cooker basin.

3 Add the macaroni pasta to the basin and stir well.

4 Put on the lid and cook on LOW for 2–3 hours.

5 When ready, remove the lid. If the sauce is really thick, stir in 50ml of milk at a time to thin it down.

6 Stir in half the cheese and sprinkle the rest of the cheese on top.

7 If you like, and if you have a flameproof basin, preheat the grill and finish the dish under the grill until the cheese is bubbling.

For the white sauce
55g butter
55g plain flour
500ml milk, plus extra
    for thinning
    (optional)
250ml water
$1/2$ tsp English mustard
Pinch of salt and freshly
    ground black pepper

For the macaroni
250g macaroni pasta
100ml milk or water
150g mature Cheddar
    cheese, grated

OPTIONS
To speed up this recipe, you can replace the white sauce with a 400g jar of white lasagne sauce, adding it directly to the slow-cooker basin at step 2 with 350ml milk, 250ml water and $1/2$ tsp English mustard.

You can vary the dish by adding vegetables such as broccoli, sweetcorn or peas. Add cooked meat – such as ham, chopped chorizo – at the end just to heat through.

A delicious dish that is ready in just a few hours, the creamy butternut squash and feta add richness to this risotto, making it popular with all the family. If you don't like feta, try it with grilled halloumi.

Butternut Squash and Feta Risotto

Serves 4

1 medium-sized butternut squash, peeled, deseeded and chopped into bite-sized pieces
1 onion, finely chopped
1 garlic clove, crushed
600ml hot vegetable stock
250g easy-cook long-grain rice
200g feta, chopped into bite-sized pieces
Salt and freshly ground black pepper

1 Put the chopped butternut squash in the slow-cooker basin and add the chopped onion and crushed garlic.

2 Pour over the hot vegetable stock, then add the rice to the basin and stir well.

3 Put the lid on tightly and cook on LOW for 3 hours until the rice is just tender and most of the liquid has been absorbed.

4 When cooked, stir the chopped feta into the risotto, season to taste with a little salt and plenty of pepper and serve.

A sumptuous dessert that is a sure-fire winner for all the family, this is not one for the faint-hearted but definitely a treat to be savoured once in a while.

Chocolate Croissant Pudding

Serves 4

1 Grease the inside of the slow-cooker basin with the butter.

2 Spread the croissants with the chocolate spread.

3 Arrange the halves around the base of the basin and sprinkle over the dark chocolate chunks.

4 In a jug, mix together the eggs, milk and vanilla sugar. Pour over the croissants. Push the croissants down so that they start to absorb the liquid.

5 Close the lid and cook on LOW for 3 hours until the liquid has been absorbed.

OPTION
Try this recipe using chocolate brioches instead of croissants, or use chocolate and hazelnut spread for a nuttier flavour.

Knob of butter
8 small croissants, cut in half
200g of chocolate spread
75g dark chocolate chunks
2 eggs, beaten
250ml semi-skimmed milk
55g vanilla sugar (or sugar plus 1 tsp vanilla extract)

The perfect autumn dish, try to use just-picked apples when they are at their best. Add all your favourite dried fruits, nuts and a few dark chocolate chips.

Baked Apples with Cinnamon Sugar

Serves 4

Knob of butter
4 large cooking apples
   (that will fit in your
   slow-cooker basin)
2 tbsp brown sugar
4 tbsp dried fruit or
   nuts of your choice
2 tsp ground cinnamon
4 tbsp golden syrup
Ice cream, cream or
   crème fraîche
   (optional), to serve

1   Turn the slow cooker on to HIGH. Place a layer of foil in the base of the basin and grease the foil with a little butter.

2   Using a chopping board and corer or small knife, core each apple to leave quite a large hole and place on the buttered foil.

3   Mix together the sugar, dried fruit and cinnamon and stuff the core of the apples right to the top.

4   Place the apples into the slow-cooker basin and then pour a tablespoon of golden syrup over each apple.

5   Put the lid on tightly and cook on HIGH for 3–4 hours. The apples will be soft with a sweet sauce of the juices.

6   Serve with ice cream, cream or crème fraîche, if you like.

This recipe uses the bain-marie cooking method (see page 15) so you will need a 600ml pudding basin which should fit in most slow-cooker basins. The sugar and juices make their own sauce in the pudding basin so don't stir them into the cake mix.

St Clement's Pudding

Serves 4

1   In a mixing bowl, cream together the butter and sugar until fluffy.

2   Pour the beaten eggs into the bowl, add the flour and fold together until well mixed.

3   Grate the zest from the orange and lemon and fold them into the cake mix.

4   Cut off the peel and as much of the pith as possible, then slice $^1/_2$ the orange and $^1/_2$ the lemon flesh. Arrange these slices on the bottom and around the inside of the pudding basin. Sprinkle the sugar all over the slices. Squeeze the juice from the other halves of lemon and orange onto the orange and lemon slices.

5   Spoon the cake mixture on top of the fruit in the pudding basin. Do not stir. Place the pudding basin into the slow-cooker basin. Fill the slow cooker with water up to about halfway up the pudding basin.

6   Place the lid on tightly and cook on HIGH for 3–4 hours. The pudding should be set and surrounded by its own sauce.

7   When ready to serve, carefully lift the pudding basin out of the slow cooker and leave to cool for a few minutes. Place a plate on top of the basin and turn out onto the plate to serve on its own or with custard or ice cream, if you like.

100g butter or
  margarine, softened
100g soft light brown
  sugar
2 eggs, beaten
100g self-raising flour
1 orange
1 lemon
50g soft light brown
  sugar
Custard or ice cream
  (optional), to serve

Chapter 5
Chop and Chuck In

This chapter does just what it says – for these recipes, all you need to do is a bit of chopping up and then all the ingredients are chucked in the slow cooker and left to do their own thing – the ultimate in convenience when you've got about five minutes to get everything ready.

This is a lovely fragrant soup with all the characteristic flavours of Thai cooking. It is made without coconut milk, which cuts down on the fat and calories dramatically, while the sweet, naturally creamy butternut squash works perfectly to give it that velvety texture. For a smooth soup, liquidize or blend before serving.

Thai-style Butternut Squash Soup

Serves 4

1 large butternut squash, peeled, deseeded and chopped
1 garlic clove, crushed
1 small potato, peeled and finely diced
$1/2$ red onion, finely diced
1 red pepper, deseeded and sliced
1 green or red finger chilli (add another for a hotter soup), deseeded and sliced
1 vegetable stock cube
800ml boiling water
1 tbsp red Thai curry paste
30g Thai jasmine rice
$1/2$ lime
2 tbsp chopped fresh coriander

1   Put the chopped butternut squash, crushed garlic, diced potato and onion, and sliced pepper and chilli in the slow-cooker basin.

2   Make up the vegetable stock with the boiling water and stock cube, then stir in the Thai curry paste. Pour over the vegetables and stir in the rice.

3   Put the lid on securely and cook on HIGH for 3 hours or on LOW for 5 hours until thick and creamy.

4   When ready to serve, finish by squeezing the lime juice into the soup and sprinkle on the fresh coriander.

A delicious fish soup classic, this is often made with seafood combinations such as smoked haddock, salmon and cod with prawn or mussels, but anything goes really as long as it's a mix. Traditionally, it is served with Gruyère cheese croûtons made with French bread, and rouille, a spiced mayonnaise.

Bouillabaisse
Serves 4

1   Rub the garlic halves around the inside of the slow-cooker basin, then crush the garlic and add it to the basin with the diced onion, celery and pepper

2   Add the chunks of fish and the seafood.

3   Stir the herbs into the hot fish stock, add the saffron and pepper, then pour over the fish and seafood.

4   Finally add the chopped tomatoes and wine and stir well.

5   Place the lid on the basin and cook on HIGH for 3–4 hours until the fish is cooked.

6   If you prefer a smooth bouillabaisse, either use a hand blender or pour the soup into the liquidizer and blend.

7   To make the rouille, mix all the ingredients together and place a spoonful in the centre of each bowl of soup to serve.

2 garlic cloves, cut in half
1 large onion, finely diced
1 celery stick, finely diced
1 red pepper, deseeded and finely diced
500g fish and seafood of your choice, skinned and cut into chunks
1 tsp Herbes de Provence
Pinch of saffron stems
1 tsp freshly ground black pepper
300ml hot fish stock
400g tin of chopped tomatoes
150ml white wine

For the rouille
1 tbsp mayonnaise
1 tsp paprika
1 tsp cayenne pepper or chilli powder

The chipotle chilli is actually a smoke-dried jalapeño pepper. It has a smoky spiciness that adds a real depth of flavour to this soup. The crushed tortilla chips serve to thicken the soup and give it a lovely texture. It needs nothing else – although you could add a dollop of soured cream.

Mexican Chipotle, Bean and Tortilla Soup

Serves 4

1 dried chipotle chilli
2 tbsp boiling water
2 celery sticks, finely chopped
1 onion, finely chopped
1/2 carrot, peeled and finely chopped
1/2 courgette, finely chopped
2 peppers (any colour), deseeded and finely chopped
1 garlic clove, crushed
1 litre boiling water
3 vegetable stock cubes
1 tsp chipotle paste
1 tsp paprika
1/2 tsp ground cumin
400g tin of mixed beans, rinsed and drained
2 x 400g tin of kidney beans, rinsed and drained
75g unsalted tortilla chips, crushed

1   Put the dried chilli to soak in 2 tbsp boiling water.

2   Put all the chopped vegetables into the slow-cooker basin, add the crushed garlic and stir well.

3   Make up the vegetable stock with the water and stock cubes, stir in the chipotle paste, then pour over the vegetables. Sprinkle the paprika and cumin on top.

4   Add the beans and the crushed tortillas and stir well.

5   Place the lid on, then cook on HIGH for 3–4 hours until soft and well blended.

Far superior to its minced beef version, the slow-cooked beef steak melts in the mouth and is a much closer match to how the American ranchers would have made their chilli over the fire.

Chilli Beef and Beans

Serves 4

1 Put the chopped onion, pepper and chilli into the slow-cooker basin with the crushed garlic. Add the beef.

2 Sprinkle on the spices, then add the drained kidney beans.

3 Make up the beef stock with the stock cubes and the boiling water, stir in the tomato purée, then pour over the top of the ingredients and stir well.

4 Cover tightly with the lid and cook on HIGH for 8–9 hours until the beef is meltingly tender.

5 Serve with boiled rice or jacket potatoes.

1 onion, finely chopped
1 red pepper, deseeded and chopped
1 red chilli, deseeded and chopped
1 garlic clove, crushed
400g beef steak, diced
1 tsp chilli powder
3 tsp ground cumin
400g tin of kidney beans, rinsed and drained
2 beef stock cubes
300ml boiling water
1 tbsp tomato purée
Boiled rice or jacket potatoes, to serve

This cut of pork is perfect for braising in cider as it slowly becomes deliciously tender. The mustard gives the savoury gravy a lovely kick and the carrot and apple make a delicious accompaniment.

Cider Braised Pork

Serves 4

1 garlic clove, cut in half
1.75kg rolled pork shoulder joint
1 tbsp wholegrain mustard
300ml hot pork stock
440ml dry cider
2 large carrots, peeled and coarsely chopped
1 large cooking apple, peeled, cored and coarsely chopped

1 Rub the garlic halves around the inside of the slow-cooker basin, then chop the garlic and add it to the basin.

2 Score the rind of the pork joint and smear the wholegrain mustard into the score marks. Place it in the slow-cooker basin.

3 Mix the hot pork stock and cider, then pour into the basin.

4 Surround the joint with the chopped carrots and apple.

5 Place the lid on the basin and cook on HIGH for 6–8 hours.

6 Lift the pork joint out carefully as it will be very tender and may fall apart. The apple and carrot can be lifted out of the stock and mashed up to make a vegetable side dish.

A speciality of the French Alps, this cheesy potato bake is delicious served with a crisp green salad. Traditionally, it is made with Reblochon cheese, a full-flavoured soft cheese. If you can't find it, use a good Brie instead. This recipe includes gammon, but it can be omitted for a vegetarian version.

Tartiflette with Gammon

Serves 4

1   Rub the garlic halves around the inside of the slow-cooker basin, then crush the garlic and add it to the basin.

2   Place the sliced potatoes and onions in layers in the basin. Pour over the water and season with salt and black pepper.

3   Place the gammon or ham slices on top of the potatoes, then finish with a layer of sliced cheese.

4   Cover with the lid and cook on LOW for 5–6 hours until the potatoes are cooked.

5   Serve large spoonfuls from the slow cooker with a crisp green salad.

1 garlic clove, cut in half
300g floury potatoes, peeled and sliced
1 onion, sliced
100ml water
Salt and freshly ground black pepper
150g gammon or thick-cut ham, sliced
300g Reblochon or Brie cheese, sliced
Crisp green salad, to serve

These chicken breasts are steamed in the wine and the juices of the leeks, leaving them succulent and delicious. Don't be tempted to add the cream before cooking; it will split and ruin the dish.

Chicken with Leeks and Mozzarella

Serves 4

500g leeks, sliced
4 back bacon rashers, rinded and chopped
1 garlic clove, crushed
4 chicken breasts
Freshly ground black pepper
2 x 100g mozzarella balls, sliced
200ml white wine
2 tbsp single cream or half-fat crème fraîche
New potatoes, to serve

1 Put the sliced leeks, chopped bacon and crushed garlic in the slow-cooker basin and mix well.

2 Lay the chicken breasts on top of the leeks and season with pepper.

3 Arrange the sliced mozzarella over the top of the chicken. Pour over the wine.

4 Place the lid on tightly and cook on LOW for 5–6 hours until the chicken is tender.

5 When ready to serve, remove the chicken breasts and stir the cream through the wine and leeks.

6 Serve with new potatoes.

Chicken thighs feature here in a well-known combination with white wine and mushrooms. Potatoes are cooked at the same time so all you need to do is cook some vegetables to complete the meal.

Chicken in White Wine and Mushrooms

Serves 4

1   Place the potatoes in the base of the slow-cooker basin and layer the sliced mushrooms and chopped onion and celery on top.

2   Season the chicken thighs with salt and pepper, then place on top of the vegetables and pour over the hot chicken stock and the white wine

3   Put the lid on tightly and cook on LOW for 6–8 hours until the chicken is falling off the bone.

4   Serve with fresh vegetables of your choice.

300g new potatoes
125g mushrooms, thickly sliced
1 onion, chopped
2 celery sticks, chopped
6–8 chicken thighs
Salt and freshly ground black pepper
300ml hot chicken stock
200ml white wine
Fresh vegetables, to serve

You can normally fit four lamb shanks in a standard-sized slow-cooker basin. This recipe works particularly well if you marinate the lamb shanks overnight, then it really is a 'chuck it all in' procedure the next morning. Remember never to refrigerate the slow-cooker basin and then put it straight into the heating vessel.

Lambs Shanks in Red Wine and Redcurrant

Serves 4

4 lamb shanks
1 onion, finely chopped
600ml hot lamb stock
200ml red wine
1 tbsp redcurrant sauce

For the marinade
1 large rosemary sprig
1 garlic clove, crushed
1/2 tsp ground cumin
1/2 tsp ground coriander
1 tbsp lemon juice
1 tbsp olive oil or cold-pressed rapeseed oil
Sea salt and freshly ground black pepper
Mashed potatoes and fresh vegetables, to serve

1 Mix together the marinade ingredients and smear over the lamb shanks. Leave to marinate in the fridge for 2 hours or preferably overnight.

2 Place the lamb shanks into the slow-cooker basin. Add the chopped onion.

3 Mix together the hot lamb stock, wine and redcurrant sauce, then pour it over the meat and and onions.

4 Place the lid on and cook on HIGH for 8 hours until the meat is perfectly tender and bathed in a rich sauce.

5 Serve with mashed potatoes and fresh vegetables.

Slow cooking the whole pepper concentrates the lovely sweet flavour and goes so well with the stuffing of lentil and vegetables and the saltiness of the halloumi.

Stuffed Peppers

Serves 4

1   Place a layer of kitchen foil in the base of the slow cooker.

2   Put the diced mushrooms, cherry tomatoes and halloumi in a separate bowl. Add the drained lentils, the passata, crushed garlic and oregano. Mix well.

3   Cut the stem off the peppers and remove the seeds and pith. Generously stuff the peppers with the mixture and place on the foil in the slow-cooker basin.

4   Put the lid on tightly and cook on LOW for 4–6 hours.

5   When ready to serve, lift the peppers out carefully as they will be very soft, using the foil to help.

6   Serve with warm crusty bread and salad.

2 mushrooms, finely diced
12 cherry tomatoes, finely diced
50g halloumi or feta cheese, diced
390g tin of green lentils, drained and rinsed
2 tbsp passata
1 garlic clove, crushed
1/2 tsp dried oregano
5–6 peppers (depending on how many will fit)
Warm crusty bread and salad, to serve

This recipe is perfect if you are preparing a big meal, such as Christmas dinner, and you have run out of oven space, saucepans or hob space. Putting the cabbage in the slow cooker is the perfect way to cook this delicious vegetable as the flavours intensify and a lovely sweetness develops.

Braised Red Cabbage

Serves 4

1 red cabbage, finely shredded
1 small onion, chopped
1 small cooking apple, peeled, cored and chopped
1 garlic clove, chopped
Grated zest and juice of 1 orange
2 tbsp balsamic vinegar
1/4 tsp freshly grated nutmeg
1 small cinnamon stick
1 tsp salt
2 tbsp soft dark brown sugar
25g raisins or sultanas (optional)
25g butter
Freshly ground black pepper

1 Put the shredded cabbage, chopped onion, apple and garlic clove into the slow-cooker basin.

2 Add the grated orange zest and juice along with the balsamic vinegar, spices and salt. Sprinkle on the sugar and stir well. Add the raisins or sultanas, if using.

3 Put the lid on and cook on LOW for 4–6 hours until the cabbage is soft and the juice rich.

4 When ready to serve, stir through the butter to give a lovely glossy finish and season well with pepper.

This clever recipe uses a similar principle to the butterscotch fondue recipe (see page 122), in which the condensed milk slowly caramelizes on the base of the slow cooker to form the toffee layer. It is really an upside-down banoffee pie.

Banoffee Pudding

Serves 4

1   Pour the condensed milk into the slow-cooker basin.

2   Put the biscuits into a freezer bag and bash with a rolling pin to crush the biscuits to form a fine crumb. Pour the crumbs into a bowl. Add the sliced bananas and turn gently to coat with the biscuit crumbs. Lift out the banana slices and place on top of the condensed milk in layers.

3   Rub the butter into the remaining biscuit crumbs and stir in the wholemeal flour.

4   Spoon the biscuit mix on top of the banana slices to completely cover the banana.

5   Place the lid on tightly and cook on HIGH for 2–3 hours.

6   Serve with a dollop of crème fraîche or whipped cream and some shavings of dark chocolate.

400g tin of condensed milk
250g digestive biscuits
4 bananas, peeled and cut into 1cm slices
28g butter
1 tbsp wholemeal flour
Crème fraîche or whipping cream, to serve
50g dark chocolate, to decorate

Chapter 6
Just Take Five

If you don't like recipes with extensive ingredients lists, then head for this chapter first because these recipes are especially for you. All these delicious meals contain only five main ingredients – I haven't included the basic seasoning in the five but I think that's fair!

This is such a simple ingredients list but the flavour is fantastic. Add more Stilton for extra blue cheese punch. Make sure you cook it on LOW as if you cook it on HIGH, the soup will split.

Leek, Potato and Stilton Soup

Serves 4

1 large leek, sliced
1 large King Edward
  potato, finely
  chopped
1 garlic clove, chopped
50g Stilton cheese,
  crumbled
1 litre hot vegetable
  stock
Salt and freshly ground
  black pepper
Crusty bread, to serve

1   Put the sliced leek, chopped potato and garlic, and crumbled cheese in the slow-cooker basin and mix together.

2   Pour over the hot vegetable stock.

3   Put the lid on tightly and cook on LOW for 4–5 hours.

4   Season to taste with salt and pepper and serve with crusty bread.

The salmon is cooked *en papillote* to seal in the moisture and flavour and to stop it disintegrating in the slow cooker, whilst the vegetables slow cook in the spices underneath. This is a slight cheat in that it has six main ingredients, but it was far too tasty a result to miss anything out just to make the right number!

Tandoori Salmon with Onions and Peppers
Serves 4

1   Rub the garlic halves around the inside of the basin, then chop the garlic finely and add it to the basin.

2   Add the chunks of pepper and onion to the basin.

3   Add 2 tsp of the tandoori curry powder to the hot fish stock and mix well, then pour over the vegetables.

4   Rub the remaining tandoori curry powder over the salmon. Tear off a piece of foil large enough to double-wrap the salmon and grease the foil. Lay the spiced salmon in the foil and double-wrap. Lay the salmon parcel on top of the vegetables.

5   Cover with the lid and cook on HIGH for 3–4 hours until the salmon flakes easily.

6   Serve with new potatoes or rice.

OPTION
Try this recipe using tikka curry powder instead of tandoori, and use sea trout fillets instead of salmon.

1 garlic clove, cut in half
2 red or green peppers, deseeded and cut into large chunks
1 red onion, cut into large chunks
5 tsp tandoori curry powder
200ml hot fish stock
500g fresh salmon fillets
A little oil, for greasing
New potatoes or boiled rice, to serve

Make sure that you buy a gammon joint that will fit in your slow cooker or you may find you have to cut it to size. The pineapple gives this a lovely sweetness which goes well with the salty gammon.

Gammon and Pineapple

Serves 4

425g tin of pineapple rings in natural juice, drained and juice reserved
300ml hot pork stock
1kg gammon joint
500g new potatoes
12 peppercorns

1   Mix the pineapple juice with the hot pork stock, then pour into the basin.

2   Place the gammon joint into the basin and surround with the new potatoes. Place half the pineapple rings and the peppercorns on top.

3   Replace the lid and cook on LOW for 6–8 hours.

4   Lift the gammon joint out carefully as it will be very tender and may fall apart.

5   Serve with the potatoes and the other half of the pineapple rings.

Another family favourite, for this recipe I use the widely available pre-made meatballs, although do use the better-quality meatballs for the best results as they don't tend to fall apart. You can, of course, make your own using minced beef, seasoning and a beaten egg.

Meatballs in Tomato Sauce

Serves 4

1   Put all the ingredients except the spaghetti and Parmesan into the slow-cooker basin and stir well.

2   Replace the lid and cook on HIGH for 4 hours or LOW for 6–8 hours.

3   Serve with spaghetti and a sprinkling of Parmesan cheese.

OPTION
Instead of the tins of tomatoes, you can make this with a 500g jar of tomato pasta sauce.

16 meatballs
2 x 400g tins of chopped tomatoes
1 small onion, finely chopped
150g vegetables of your choice (red pepper, mushroom, courgette, carrot), finely chopped
$1/2$ tsp dried oregano
Spaghetti and grated Parmesan cheese, to serve

Pork chops can become dry, tough and flavourless when cooked in the oven or under a grill, but slow cooking them in ginger beer ensures that they are succulent and tasty every time.

Pork in Ginger and Apple
Serves 4

1 cooking apple, peeled, cored and cut into bite-sized pieces
1 small onion, cut into bite-sized pieces
600–700g pork chops (4–6 chops)
Salt and freshly ground black pepper
1 pork stock cube
50ml boiling water
500ml ginger beer
Potatoes of your choice, to serve
Sage leaves to garnish

1 Put the pieces of apple and onion into the slow-cooker basin.

2 Season the pork chops with salt and pepper, then lay them on top of the apple and onion.

3 Dissolve the stock cube in the boiling water, stir in the ginger beer, then pour into the basin.

4 Put the lid on tightly and cook on LOW for 6–8 hours until the pork chops are tender.

5 Serve with your favourite style of potatoes and garnish with sage leaves.

As venison sausages are darker than pork sausages, it doesn't matter so much if you don't brown them off prior to slow cooking them.

Venison Sausage Cassoulet

Serves 4

1 Mix together the chopped tomatoes and the pasta sauce in the slow-cooker basin.

2 Add the smoked paprika and stir well.

3 Add the cannellini beans to the basin.

4 Place the venison sausages in the basin, making sure they are covered with the tomato sauce.

5 Put the lid on tightly and cook on LOW for 6–8 hours until the sausages are cooked through.

6 Serve with creamy mashed potato and wholegrain mustard.

400g tin of chopped tomatoes
320g jar of tomato pasta sauce
1 tsp smoked paprika
400g tin of cannellini beans, drained and rinsed
12 venison sausages
Creamy mashed potato and wholegrain mustard, to serve

This pub classic is so very simple in a slow cooker, and only takes about five minutes to prepare. Served with jacket potato or wedges, it makes a delicious meal – who needs to venture out!

Hunter's Chicken

Serves 4

4 chicken breasts
8 back bacon rashers, rind removed
450g jar of barbecue sauce
200ml hot water
100g Cheddar cheese, grated
Chunky chips and vegetables, to serve

1 Lay out the first chicken breast and wrap 2 bacon rashers around the breast so that it is covered. Secure with half a cocktail stick. Repeat for the other 3 breasts. Arrange the chicken breasts in the base of the slow-cooker basin.

2 Tip out the barbecue sauce into a jug, add the hot water and stir well until blended. Pour over the chicken.

3 Place the lid on tightly and cook on HIGH for 6–8 hours until the sauce is bubbling and the chicken succulent.

4 Heat the grill. Using tongs, lift the chicken pieces out of the basin and transfer them to a flameproof dish. Sprinkle the cheese on top of the chicken and grill until the cheese is bubbling. Remove the cocktail sticks. Put some of the sauce from the pot into a jug and serve on the side.

5 Serve with chips and vegetables.

A classic marriage of two great Spanish exports, mushrooms and red wine, this dish makes a good-size tapas or is also a tasty accompaniment to a steak dinner.

Mushrooms in Rioja

Serves 4

1 Place a sheet of kitchen foil in the slow-cooker basin, then place the mushrooms, overlapping, in the basin.

2 Pour the red wine over the mushrooms and sprinkle with the garlic and smoked paprika. Season with pepper.

3 Place the lid on tightly and cook on LOW for 6–7 hours until the mushrooms are soft.

6 large flat mushrooms, peeled
125ml Rioja wine
1 garlic clove, crushed
$^1/_2$ tsp smoked paprika
Freshly ground black pepper

You will be forgiven for having a little taste of this just to make sure it is suitable for your guests or family. Rich and creamy with that delicious salty-sweet combination, this is a fabulous dipping sauce for fruit or, when warm, a pouring sauce for ice cream.

Butterscotch Fondue

Serves 4

130g soft light brown sugar
100g butter
1 tsp vanilla extract
100ml golden syrup
Fresh fruit pieces and shortbread fingers, to serve

1 Turn the slow cooker on to HIGH.

2 Put all the ingredients except the fruit and biscuits into the slow-cooker basin and mix well. Stir the mixture until the butter melts and the sugar starts to dissolve.

3 Put the lid on tightly, switch to LOW and cook for 3 hours.

4 The fondue mix may look a bit lumpy, but a few seconds in a blender or liquidizer will make it fabulously smooth.

5 Serve with fresh fruit pieces and shortbread fingers.

This rich dessert is made in tiny espresso cups and cooked using the bain marie method (see page 15), in which the dessert is cooked in cups immersed in hot water. They are very indulgent so espresso cups are the perfect size!

Rich Chocolate Cups
Makes enough to fill 6 espresso cups

1   Melt the butter and chocolate in a bowl set over a saucepan of hot water. Stir the mixture regularly and do not let the water boil. Remove the bowl from the saucepan and leave to cool.

2   Whisk together the eggs and sugar, and the instant coffee, if using.

3   When the chocolate has cooled off a little, mix in the egg and sugar mixture and stir well.

4   Pour the chocolate mix into 6 espresso cups and place them in the slow-cooker basin. Pour enough boiling water into the slow-cooker basin to come halfway up the sides of the espresso cups.

5   Put the lid on tightly and cook on LOW for 3 hours until set and slightly risen.

6   Serve warm with a small dollop of fresh cream or a chocolate coffee bean on the top.

50g butter
150g dark chocolate
2 eggs
50g soft dark brown sugar
2 tsp instant coffee granules (optional to make a Mocha Chocolate Cup)

Chapter 7
Store Cupboard

There are times when you just can't get to the shops but if you keep a well-stocked store cupboard, you will always be able to put something tasty together. Here's a batch of recipes for which you should have everything in the cupboard, freezer or vegetable box to ensure that you can always make a lovely meal.

There are quite literally thousands of variations on the theme of minestrone soup, but essentially it is a leftovers soup so you can really chuck in anything you want within reason. It even varies with its inclusion of pasta, with some regions using potatoes instead and some not even adding tomatoes! I have used macaroni pasta as it is thicker and therefore stands up to the slow-cooking process.

Minestrone Soup

Serves 4

1 garlic clove, cut in half
2 celery sticks, finely chopped
2 onions, finely chopped
1 carrot, peeled and finely chopped
1 leek, finely chopped
400g tin of cannellini beans, drained and rinsed
800ml hot vegetable stock
400g tin of chopped tomatoes
1/2 tsp dried oregano
75g macaroni or 100g new potatoes, cut into chunks
Salt and freshly ground black pepper

1 Rub the garlic halves around the inside of the slow-cooker basin, then finely chop the garlic and add it to the basin.

2 Add the chopped vegetables and the beans and stir together.

3 Pour in the hot vegetable stock, add the chopped tomatoes, oregano and pasta or potatoes and stir well.

4 Place the lid on the basin and cook on HIGH for 3–4 hours to a thick soup.

5 Season to taste with salt and pepper before serving.

A classic Italian bean soup with rich tomato flavours that develop over time. With slow-release energy from the beans and lentils, this soup will leave you feeling full for hours.

Tuscan Bean Soup

Serves 4

1   Rub the garlic halves around the inside of the slow-cooker basin, then finely chop the garlic and add it to the basin with the chopped pepper and the beans.

2   Stir the sun-dried tomato paste into the hot vegetable stock, then pour it into the basin.

3   Finally add the lentils and chopped tomatoes and stir well.

4   Place the lid on the basin and cook on HIGH for 3–4 hours to a rich soup.

5   Season to taste with salt and pepper before serving and garnish with fresh basil leaves.

1 garlic clove, cut in half
1 red pepper, deseeded and finely chopped
2 x 400g tins of mixed beans of your choice, drained and rinsed
2 tbsp sun-dried tomato paste
500ml hot vegetable stock
50g red lentils
400g tin of chopped tomatoes
Salt and freshly ground black pepper
Fresh basil leaves to garnish

Pisto is the Spanish version of ratatouille, and this quick and easy recipe makes a great supper dish. Served as tapas or as a meal with a Spanish tortilla or some Spanish potatoes a lo Pobre (see page 136).

Prawn and Chickpea Pisto

Serves 4

225g frozen king
   prawns
400g tin of chickpeas,
   rinsed and drained
400g tin of ratatouille
400g tin of chopped
   tomatoes
1 garlic clove, crushed
1 tsp smoked paprika
Salt and freshly ground
   black pepper

1 Lay the prawns out in a shallow dish and cover with cold water to defrost. This will only take a few minutes.

2 Put the chickpeas, ratatouille and tomatoes in the slow-cooker basin. Stir in the garlic and smoked paprika.

3 When defrosted, add the prawns.

4 Place the lid on tightly and cook on LOW for 3–4 hours until the chickpeas are soft.

5 Season to taste with salt and pepper before serving.

OPTION
For a vegetarian version, just omit the prawns!

This dish really concentrates down the delicious pepper flavours with the sweetness of the honey and the apricots. As well as a tasty summer salad dish, this makes a lovely vegetarian option or a great side dish for a Moroccan meal.

Moroccan Peppers
Serves 4

1   Remove the peppers from the freezer and spread them out on a baking tray to defrost.

2   Put the chopped onion, crushed garlic and chopped apricots in the slow-cooker basin. Add the peppers.

3   Add the honey and the harissa paste to the boiling water, stir well, then pour into the basin.

4   Put the lid on the basin and cook on LOW for 6–8 hours until the peppers are soft and rich.

5   Serve with flatbread and natural yoghurt drizzled over the top.

OPTION
Add a can of drained of chick peas for a more hearty vegetarian meal. You could also add 225g cooked prawns for the last half an hour of cooking.

500g frozen sliced peppers
1 small onion, chopped
1 garlic clove, crushed
75g ready-to-eat dried apricots, chopped
1 tbsp clear honey
1 tsp harissa paste (or 2 tsp for extra spice)
100ml boiling water
Flatbread and natural yoghurt, to serve

This translates literally as 'poor man's potatoes' but don't let that put you off! It's a really tasty way to serve potatoes, either as a tapas dish or as an accompaniment to a meal. The potatoes are soft and moist and infused with the flavours of the pepper and garlic.

Spanish Potatoes a lo Pobre

Serves 4

1 tbsp olive oil
150g frozen sliced peppers
1 onion, chopped
1 garlic clove, crushed
4–5 floury potatoes, peeled and thickly sliced
1 tsp smoked paprika
Pinch of salt

1   Sprinkle the olive oil over the base of the slow-cooker basin.

2   Put the peppers in the bottom of the basin and turn the slow cooker onto HIGH so that they start to defrost. Place the chopped onion and crushed garlic on top of the peppers. Arrange the sliced potatoes on top.

3   Season with the smoked paprika and the salt.

4   Place the lid on tightly and cook on HIGH for 4–5 hours until the potatoes are soft and full of flavour.

OPTIONS
Add a large handful of chopped spicy chorizo for a more substantial dish. It is also traditional to crack an egg or two on top of this dish, and you can replicate this by frying two eggs on the hob and serving the dish with the eggs on top.

An easy supper option for the family straight from the cupboard. Remember to use the easy-cook rice and keep to the timings so that the rice doesn't go too sticky.

Pea and Wild Mushroom Risotto

Serves 4

1   Soak the dried mushrooms in the hot vegetable stock for about 30 minutes.

2   Add the frozen peas.

3   Put the chopped onion and crushed garlic into the slow-cooker basin. Add the mushrooms in stock and peas, then add the rice and stir well.

4   Put the lid on tightly and cook on LOW for 3 hours until the rice is just tender to the bite.

5   When cooked, season to taste with a little salt and pepper and serve sprinkled with grated Parmesan cheese.

OPTION
Use different varieties of dried mushrooms, or use green beans instead of peas. For a non-vegetarian option, add cooked ham or chicken pieces at the end and heat through.

30g dried porcini
    mushrooms
600ml hot vegetable
    stock
100g frozen peas
1 onion, finely chopped
1 garlic clove, crushed
300g easy-cook long-
    grain rice
Salt and freshly ground
    black pepper
25g Parmesan cheese,
    grated

The unrefined sugars and treacle in this recipe give this a lovely dark brown colour that means it can be slow cooked without looking white and pale. The moist cake is delicious, and if you store it wrapped in clingfilm in an airtight container, the stickiness will improve over the next few days.

Sticky Ginger Cake

Serves 4

75g butter or margarine, plus extra for greasing
75g soft dark brown sugar
2 tsp ground ginger
$1/2$ tsp ground cinnamon
1 tbsp freshly grated root ginger
2 eggs
2 tbsp black treacle
2 tbsp golden syrup
1 tsp vanilla extract
175g self-raising flour
$1/2$ tsp baking powder
Custard or ice cream, to serve (optional)

1 Switch the slow cooker onto HIGH. Grease the basin and line with some baking parchment (it helps when lifting the cake out).

2 In a bowl, cream together the butter or margarine and sugar, then add the dry spices and mix well.

3 Beat the eggs in a jug and add the treacle, syrup and vanilla extract. Stir well.

4 Add the flour, baking powder and grated ginger to the bowl, pour in the contents of the jug and stir well. Pour the mix into the slow-cooker basin and level off the surface.

5 Turn the slow cooker to LOW, cover with the lid and cook for 3 hours until just firm to the touch.

6 When ready, lift out the cake and either serve there and then with custard or ice cream or leave to cool and have with a nice cup of tea.

The polenta in this recipe gives this moist cake a fabulous texture. It can be served either with tea, or with cream or ice cream as a dessert.

Lemon and Polenta cake

1 Line the slow-cooker basin with baking parchment or greaseproof paper and grease well.

2 Lay the lemon slices on the base of the slow-cooker basin and sprinkle the brown sugar and lemon zest over the top of them. Add the lemon juice to the basin.

3 Cream together the butter and caster sugar in another bowl until light and creamy. Add the honey and the beaten eggs, then add the flour and polenta and fold in using a large metal spoon. Spoon the cake mixture over the top of the lemon and smooth over gently.

4 Place the lid on tightly and cook on LOW for 3–4 hours until springy to the touch.

5 When cooked, leave to cool for a few minutes, then remove the lining paper and cake from the basin and tip upside-down onto a serving plate. Remove the paper and serve warm with a swirl of whipped cream.

125g butter, softened, plus extra for greasing
1 lemon, sliced
2 tbsp dark brown sugar
Grated zest and juice of 1 lemon
125g caster sugar
1 tbsp clear honey
2 eggs, beaten
75g self-raising flour
50g fine polenta
Whipped cream to serve

Slow-cooked milk puddings seem to be a thing of the past. However, this recipe was developed on the insistence of my husband who frequently reminisced about the comfort of coming home and tucking into a lovely warm bowl of macaroni pudding. Rest assured, the yummy caramelized edge still develops in the slow cooker.

Spiced Macaroni Pudding

Serves 4

100g macaroni pasta
50g caster sugar
1 tsp vanilla extract
1 tsp mixed spice
500ml milk
1 tbsp double cream,
  golden syrup or
  raspberry jam
  (optional)

1 Add all of the ingredients except the cream, syrup or jam to the slow-cooker basin and mix together well, stirring until the sugar has dissolved.

2 Place the lid on tightly and cook on LOW for 4–5 hours.

3 For an extra indulgent touch, stir through a spoonful of double cream, golden syrup or raspberry jam – but not all three!

Chapter 8
Cheap Eats

This is nothing to do with the time constraints of a busy lifestyle, but very important when we are all trying to eat well on a reduced budget. You'll find this chapter features cheaper cuts of meat, leftovers, or ingredients that are available very cheaply, so all these recipes are particularly economical to make.

Red split lentils are so cheap to buy and are a healthy non-meat protein source. Make this soup as spicy as you want by increasing the amount of cayenne pepper you use.

Spicy Lentil and Bacon Soup

Serves 4

1 onion, finely chopped
4 smoked back bacon rashers, rinded and chopped
600ml hot vegetable or chicken stock
400g tin of chopped tomatoes
$1/2$ tsp cayenne pepper
1 tsp Worcestershire sauce
100g split red lentils

1   Put the chopped onion and bacon into the slow-cooker basin.

2   Pour in the hot vegetable or chicken stock and add the chopped tomatoes. Add the cayenne and Worcestershire sauce and stir well.

3   Finally add the lentils and stir again.

4   Put the lid on tightly and cook on HIGH for 3–4 hours. For a smoother soup, blend to your desired consistency.

This really is a surprise to all who have tasted it, as they thought it sounded boring, but there is something magical about the sweet onion flavour and the creamy cannellini beans that are very tasty indeed.

White Bean and Onion Soup

Serves 4

1. Put the sliced onions and chopped bacon into the slow-cooker basin. Add the diced potato, crushed garlic and cumin.

2. Pour in the hot chicken stock and the beans and stir gently.

3. Put the lid on tightly and cook on HIGH for 3–4 hours.

4. Season to taste with salt and pepper. Blend for a smoother consistency.

3 large white onions, thinly sliced

2 smoked back bacon rashers, rinded and chopped

1 medium-sized floury potato, peeled and finely diced

1 garlic clove, crushed

$1/2$ tsp ground cumin

1 litre hot chicken stock

400g tin of cannellini beans, drained and rinsed

Salt and freshly ground black pepper

This is a great way to cook ribs in an efficient 'hands off' way. You don't even need to marinate them as they absorb all the flavours as they slow cook. The meat falls off the bone and is tasty and tender. These next two recipes are classic styles of ribs flavourings to try.

Sticky Five-spice Ribs

Serves 4

For the Chinese-style rub
1 tsp freshly ground black pepper
1/2 tsp salt
1/2 tsp garlic salt
1/2 tsp ground cumin
2 tsp Chinese five-spice powder
2 tsp paprika

750g–1kg pork ribs
300ml hot pork stock
1 tbsp soy sauce
1 tbsp tomato purée
2 tbsp golden syrup
2 tsp cornflour

1   Combine the dry rub ingredients and rub over the pork ribs. Leave to marinate whilst you make the sauce.

2   Mix the hot pork stock with the soy sauce, tomato purée and golden syrup. Pour the sauce into the slow-cooker basin. Place the ribs on top of the sauce.

3   Place the lid on tightly and cook on LOW for 5–6 hours until the ribs are tender.

4   To thicken the sauce, remove the ribs from the basin and pour the sauce into a saucepan. Remove a few tablespoons to mix with the cornflour to a smooth paste, then return that to the sauce and heat gently until thickened, stirring continuously. Pour some of the thick sauce over the ribs to serve and put the rest into a jug to serve separately.

Slow cook these ribs all day and finish them off on the barbecue in the evening for a perfect summer's evening feast.

Smoky Barbecue Pork Ribs

Serves 4

1 Combine the dry rub ingredients and rub over the pork ribs. Leave to marinate whilst you make the sauce.

2 Pour the hot water into a jug, add all the sauces and mix well. Pour the sauce into the slow-cooker basin and add the diced onion. Place the ribs on top of the sauce.

3 Place the lid on tightly and cook on LOW for 5–6 hours until the meat is tender.

4 To thicken the sauce, remove the ribs from the basin, pour the sauce into a saucepan and remove a few tablespoons to mix with the cornflour. Combine with the rest of the sauce and heat up until thickened, stirring continuously. Pour some over the ribs and put the rest into a jug to serve separately.

750g–1kg pork ribs

For the barbecue rub
2 tsp smoked paprika
2 tsp brown sugar
2 tsp salt
1 tsp cayenne pepper
   or chilli powder
   (increase if you like
   them spicy)
1 garlic clove, crushed

For the sauce
150ml hot water
3 tbsp tomato sauce
3 tbsp barbecue sauce
2 tsp Worcestershire
   sauce
1 tsp chilli sauce
1 onion, finely diced
2 tsp cornflour

In Mexico, this pulled pork dish is served wrapped in banana leaves and garnished with pickled red onions, but any of your favourite Mexican accompaniments will taste great. If you can't get hold of achiote, replace it with paprika or ground pimento.

Pulled Citrus Pork

Serves 4

1 tsp ground cumin
1 tsp ground coriander
1 tsp chilli powder
1/2 tsp freshly ground
   black pepper
2 tbsp achiote
   (Mexican annatto), or
   paprika or ground
   pimento
3 garlic cloves, crushed
100ml lime juice
1.5kg rolled pork
   shoulder
250ml orange juice
1 tsp dried oregano
Flour tortillas, salsa,
   guacamole and
   salad, to serve

1 Mix together the spices with the crushed garlic and the lime juice to make a paste.

2 Score the surface of the pork, down through the skin to the meat, and place in the slow-cooker basin. Smear the pork with the spice paste, getting as much into the score marks as possible.

3 Pour the orange juice around the meat and sprinkle the dried oregano on the top.

4 Place the lid on the slow cooker and cook on LOW for 8–10 hours until the pork is falling-apart soft.

5 When cooked, lift the pork out carefully, as it will be very soft, and place on a large plate. Remove the outer layer of skin and fat and any string.

6 Using two forks, pull the pieces of pork apart and start to break down the meat pieces into smaller fibres. Remove any internal layers of fat.

7 Spoon 8 tablespoons of the cooking juice back over the pulled pork and cover with foil until ready to serve.

8 Serve with flour tortillas, salsa, guacamole and salad.

This is a great way to use up that chunk of roast pork left over from Sunday lunch, making it a perfect dish for the start of the week. Serve with pasta or rice or with a jacket potato.

Leftover Pork Roast Ragu

Serves 4

1 Put the diced celery, carrot and onion and any other vegetables into the slow-cooker basin.

2 Add the cubes of meat and slivers of bacon. Pour over the passata, add the herbs and stir well.

3 Place the lid on tightly and cook on LOW for 6–8 hours until tender.

4 Serve with pasta, rice or jacket potatoes and sprinkle with parmesan.

1 celery stick, finely diced
1 carrot, peeled and finely diced
1 onion, finely diced
$1/2$ red pepper, deseeded and finely diced (optional)
$1/2$ red courgette, finely diced (optional)
300–400g roast pork, chopped into 1cm cubes
2 smoked bacon rashers, rinded and cut into thin slivers
500g passata
$1/2$ tsp Italian mixed herbs
Pasta, rice or jacket potatoes, to serve
Grated parmesan

Allspice is a key flavour in this intense spicy jerk seasoning that goes so well with the chicken to make this Caribbean treat.

Jerk Chicken

Serves 4

1 large onion, grated
2 spring onions, chopped
3 garlic cloves, chopped
1 red chilli, deseeded and chopped
Juice and zest of 1 lime
1 tbsp soft light brown sugar
1 tbsp grated fresh ginger root
2 tbsp soy sauce
2 tbsp white wine vinegar
100ml orange juice
2 tbsp lemon juice
2 tsp allspice
8 chicken drumsticks
Boiled rice and red beans, to serve

1   Put the grated onion into the slow-cooker basin and add the chopped spring onions, garlic and chilli.

2   Add all the remaining ingredients except the chicken to the vegetables and mix well.

3   Put the drumsticks into the basin, making sure that the meat parts are in the sauce and the legs are sticking out.

4   Put the lid on and cook on HIGH for 3–4 hours until the chicken is falling off the drumsticks.

5   Serve with boiled rice and red beans.

Chicken thighs are a lovely cheap cut of meat, full of flavour, and after 8 hours in the slow cooker, the meat falls off the bone easily. As well as pasta, this versatile dish can be served with rice, mashed potato or as jacket potato filling.

Tuscan-style Chicken

Serves 4

1 Put the chopped onion, celery and courgette in the slow-cooker basin and add the sliced pepper, crushed garlic, oregano and drained beans. Mix well.

2 Add the tins of chopped tomatoes or chopped and cherry tomatoes. Crumble in the chicken stock cube and mix well again.

3 Trim the excess skin and fat from the chicken thighs and add the thighs to the basin. Stir carefully, so that there is tomato juice on the chicken.

4 Put the lid on securely and cook on LOW for 8 hours until the chicken is tender.

5 At the end of cooking, stir through the black olives and serve with pasta or chunks of bread.

1 red onion, finely chopped
1 celery stick, finely chopped
$1/2$ courgette, finely chopped
$1/2$ red pepper, deseeded and sliced, or 100g frozen sliced peppers
1 garlic clove, crushed
1 tsp dried oregano
400g tin of cannellini beans, drained and rinsed
2 x 400g tins of chopped tomatoes or chopped tomatoes and cherry tomatoes
1 chicken stock cube
6–8 chicken thighs
100g pitted black olives
Pasta or chunks of bread, to serve

The lamb just falls apart and melts in the mouth when cooked in the slow cooker, while the suggested accompaniments make this a real Greek feast.

Garlic and Rosemary Shoulder of Lamb
Serves 4

2 garlic cloves, cut in half
2 tsp chopped fresh rosemary
2 tsp garlic salt
1 tsp dried mixed herbs
1 tsp freshly ground black pepper
750g boneless lamb shoulder
500g potatoes, peeled and cut into 5mm slices
1 small onion, chopped
300ml hot lamb stock
Feta, tomato and cucumber salad and warmed pitta bread, to serve

1   Rub one of the garlic cloves around the slow-cooker basin, then chop finely.

2   Mix all the dry herbs and spices together and rub into the lamb.

3   Line the slow-cooker basin with the potato slices, making a few layers.

4   Place the lamb on top of the potatoes and surround with the chopped garlic and onion. Pour over the hot lamb stock.

5   Place the lid on tightly and cook on HIGH for 6–8 hours until the lamb is easy to pull from the bone.

6   Serve with the salad and warm pitta bread.

This lovely, rich, nutty sauce is delicious with the slow-cooked lamb. As lamb is a fatty meat, it is worth the effort to cut off the fat before cooking as it will result in a much better dish and benefit your health too.

Oriental Spiced Lamb

Serves 4

1   In the slow-cooker basin, combine all of the spices, pastes and liquids, finishing with the grated onion on top. Stir well to make a thick paste.

2   Add the trimmed and diced lamb and coat it well with the paste.

3   Place the lid on the cooker and cook on LOW for 6–8 hours until the lamb is tender.

4   If you want to crisp up the lamb and serve it more like satay skewers, place the cubes of lamb onto skewers and grill for a few minutes under a hot grill.

5   Serve with Thai fragrant rice or noodles.

2 tbsp tamarind paste
2 tbsp peanut butter (crunchy or smooth)
3 garlic cloves, crushed
3 tbsp soy sauce
2 tbsp lemon juice
2 red chillies, finely chopped
1 tbsp soft light brown sugar
1 onion, grated
800g stewing lamb, trimmed and cubed
Thai fragrant rice or noodles, to serve

Thick and creamy yellow split lentils and juicy tomatoes make this a delicious meal on its own or as an accompaniment to your favourite curry.

Tomato and Lentil Dhal

Serves 4

3 fresh tomatoes, coarsely chopped
250g yellow split lentils
2 garlic cloves, crushed
1/4 tsp ground turmeric
1 tsp ground coriander
1 tsp ground cumin
2 tbsp lemon juice
700ml hot vegetable stock
1 tbsp chopped fresh coriander
Salt

1   Keep back one of the tomatoes and the fresh coriander to stir in at the end of cooking. Place all the remaining ingredients in the slow-cooker basin and stir well.

2   Place the lid on tightly and cook on LOW for 3–4 hours until the lentils are cooked down to a thick texture.

3   At the end of cooking, season to taste with a little salt and garnish with the tomato and coriander.

There is amazingly little liquid added to this dish because the vegetables contain all the liquid we need to make this rich, succulent vegetable dish. It is perfect as a side dish or you can add feta cheese or grilled, chopped halloumi at the end of cooking for a vegetarian meal option.

Mediterranean Balsamic Vegetables

Serves 4

1   Rub the garlic around the slow-cooker basin, then crush the garlic and add it to the basin.

2   Add the vegetables, sprinkle over the vinegar, add the oregano and pesto and stir very well.

3   Place the lid on tightly and cook on LOW for 8–9 hours until the vegetables are tender.

4   Garnish with the fresh herbs and serve.

2 garlic cloves, cut in half
1kg vegetables (tomatoes, peppers, courgette, onions, shallots, aubergine, mushrooms, olives), chopped into large chunks
2 tbsp balsamic vinegar
$1/2$ tsp dried oregano
1 tbsp pesto
Fresh basil and thyme to garnish

There is nothing more comforting than a bowl of rice pudding and this chocolate orange version is scrumptious. Add the cream for an extra indulgence.

Chocolate Orange Rice Pudding

Serves 4

2 oranges
150g easy-cook rice
700ml milk
50g caster sugar
100g dark chocolate
    chips
100ml single cream
    (optional)
Grated dark chocolate

1   Zest the oranges, then cut off the skin and pith and chop up the flesh. Remove the central pithy core of the orange segments. Add the flesh to the slow-cooker basin.

2   Add the rice, milk and sugar and stir well.

3   Place the lid on and cook on LOW for 4–5 hours until thick and creamy.

4   When cooked, stir in the dark chocolate chips and the cream, if using.

5   Sprinkle over some grated dark chocolate.

OPTION
Leave out the orange and chocolate and add 1 tsp cinnamon for a traditional version of rice pudding.

Don't be tempted to stir in the toffee apple syrup; it is poured over the top of the sponge mix and will seep through during cooking to make a toffee sauce at the bottom that is very sticky and absolutely delicious.

Toffee Apple Pudding

Serves 4

1 Grease the slow-cooker basin with the oil.

2 In a bowl, cream together the sugar and butter or margarine.

3 Beat the eggs and add to the creamed mixture along with the flour and vanilla extract. Stir in the apple pieces, then spoon the cake mixture into the basin. Smooth over to cover the base.

4 In a saucepan, heat the apple juice, golden syrup and sugar. Stir until the sugar dissolves, then bring to the boil. Remove from the heat.

5 Pour the toffee apple syrup over the cake mix and put the lid on tightly.

6 Cook on HIGH for 3 hours until the pudding is just springy to the touch.

7 Serve warm from the slow-cooker basin with vanilla ice cream.

1 tbsp vegetable oil
200g soft light brown sugar
200g butter or margarine, softened
3 medium eggs
200g self-raising flour
1 tsp vanilla extract
2 eating apples, peeled, cored and chopped into bite-sized pieces
300ml apple juice
100g golden syrup
100g soft light brown sugar
Vanilla ice cream, to serve

Chapter 9
The Weekender

With recipes that are a little more involved, or perhaps require more preparation or attention, this chapter is for when time is not quite as pressured. This chapter also includes recipes that are bases for other recipes, such as stock.

This dish takes some pre-preparation either the day before or evening before, but this time is well spent as it maximizes the fragrant elements of the layers in this wonderful traditional feasting dish. As it is quite a dry dish, I thoroughly recommend serving it with a vegetable curry.

Layered Chicken Biryani

Serves 4

500g chicken breast,
 cut into chunks

For the marinade
1 tbsp crushed garlic
1 tbsp grated fresh
 root ginger
2 tsp chilli powder
1 tsp garam masala
1/2 tsp salt
1/4 tsp ground turmeric
1 tbsp lemon juice

For the onion layer
2 tbsp vegetable oil
2 large onions, thinly
 sliced

For the basmati rice
 layer
300g easy-cook
 basmati rice
1 tsp salt
1 bay leaf
2 cardamom pods
300ml boiling water

For the saffron milk
300ml milk
12 strands of saffron

4 tbsp chopped fresh
 coriander
Vegetable curry and
 naan bread, to serve

The day or evening before

1 Place the chicken chunks in a bowl. Mix together all the ingredients for the chicken marinade and mix with the chicken, ensuring it is covered with the marinade. Cover and store overnight in the fridge.

2 Heat the oil in a frying pan and fry the sliced onions until golden brown. Leave to cool, then place them in the fridge in another container.

3 Put the rice, salt, bay leaf and cardamom pods in a bowl and cover with the boiling water. Leave overnight in the fridge to soak up the water.

4 Measure out the milk in a jug, heat until lukewarm, then add the saffron strands. Stir well and leave overnight in the fridge.

On the day

5 Place half the marinated chicken pieces on the base of the slow-cooker basin, layer half the onions on top and sprinkle over 1 tbsp chopped coriander leaves. Layer half of the basmati rice on top.

6 Repeat with the other half of the ingredients, remembering to sprinkle the chopped coriander leaves on the onion layer.

7 Pour over the saffron milk, put the lid on and cook on LOW for 8 hours until the rice is cooked.

8 When cooked, tip out onto a large serving dish and sprinkle on the rest of the chopped coriander.

9 Serve with vegetable curry and naan bread.

This dish takes its inspiration from the Texas smoke houses found all over the state. You may find that brisket comes as a rolled joint, but for this recipe the beef needs to be unrolled and cooked as a strip joint. You can buy Texan-style barbecue rubs or just make it up yourself depending on which flavours you like, but I have included a simple recipe here for you to try.

Texas-style Barbecue Beef

Serves 4

1. Rub the spice mix into the surface of the beef and leave to marinate for at least 15 minutes.

2. Place the chopped onions, crushed garlic and the other vegetables in the bottom of the slow-cooker basin.

3. Stir the barbecue sauce and brown sugar into the beef stock, then pour over the vegetable layer in the slow-cooker basin.

4. Sear the beef either in a hot pan or under a hot grill and place on top of the layer of vegetables and hot beef stock.

5. Put on the lid and cook on HIGH for 7–8 hours until the beef is easy to pull apart.

6. Remove the beef from the slow cooker and place in a serving dish.

7. Pour the liquid into a frying pan and simmer for a few minutes until the sauce has thickened up. Add the vinegar, then pour over the beef.

8. Serve with a bun and your favourite salad.

For a simple rub
1 tbsp caster sugar
2 tsp salt
1 tsp mixed spice
2 tsp garlic salt
1 tsp onion powder
4 tsp smoked paprika

For the beef
900g beef brisket
2 tbsp barbecue rub
2 onions, coarsely chopped
1 garlic clove, crushed
2–3 pieces of root vegetables or celery, coarsely chopped
2 tbsp barbecue sauce
2 tbsp soft light brown sugar or golden syrup
200ml hot beef stock
2 tbsp of malt vinegar
Bread rolls and salad to serve

There are many variations to making salt beef, the more traditional involving brining the meat for a few days in the fridge before soaking and then slow cooking the beef. Some methods include salt petre but it is not necessary. The brining process does partially preserve the beef, but this delicious meat won't last long enough for that to be an issue, so use within three days of cooking. If you don't have time to brine, just go ahead and slow-cook the brisket as described in the second half of this recipe. It's still a delicious dish and the melt-in-the-mouth beef is fabulous.

Salt Beef Brisket

Serves 4

1kg rolled beef brisket

For brining
400g salt
200g sugar
1 bay leaf
12 peppercorns
6 coriander seeds
Other flavourings such
   as chilli, garlic,
   ginger, allspice,
   cloves can be used
   according to your
   taste
2 litres water

For slow cooking
1 tsp cumin
1 tsp paprika
1 tsp ground black
   pepper
2 garlic cloves, crushed
2 carrots, peeled and
   chopped
1 celery stick, chopped
1 onion, chopped
2 tsp Worcestershire
   sauce
300ml hot beef stock

1 Place the brine ingredients in a large saucepan and mix so that the salt and sugar dissolve. Bring to the boil and simmer for a few minutes. Leave to cool.

2 Place the piece of beef in a large plastic bowl (one that will fit in your fridge) and pour over the liquid so that the meat is completely immersed. If you need to top up with a bit more cold water, then that is fine; it's more important that it is covered.

3 Leave to brine for up to 7 days (the longer you leave it, the deeper the brine is able to penetrate and the more flavoursome the result).

4 After brining, remove from the fridge and rinse. Place back in the bowl, cover with cold water and leave to soak overnight.

5 Mix the spices and garlic together and rub all over the surface of the beef, then place it in the slow-cooker basin and surround with the vegetables.

6 Add the Worcestershire sauce to the hot beef stock, then pour into the basin.

7 Put the lid on tightly and cook on LOW for 8–10 hours.

8 When cooked, lift out carefully and place on a dish, then leave to rest for a few minutes before slicing.

OPTION
Place 500g of new potatoes at the bottom of the slow cooker and place the beef on top. They make a delicious accompaniment to the salt beef.

Don't be put off by the long list of ingredients! They are all contained in the spice paste so if you like this dish, then I would recommend making a bulk quantity of paste and freezing it in ice cube trays so that you can use it whenever you fancy. Or, you can now buy pre-made pastes if you don't have the time or the ingredients.

Malaysian Beef Rendang

Serves 4

1 Chop all the paste ingredients and blitz in a food processor to form a paste. Add to the slow-cooker basin.

2 Add the beef and coat in the spice paste.

3 Add the lime juice, sugar and coconut milk and stir well so that it is all mixed.

4 Put on the lid and cook on LOW for 8–10 hours until the beef is tender.

5 Serve with jasmine rice.

For the paste
4 garlic cloves
6cm piece of fresh root ginger, peeled and sliced
2 stems of lemongrass, outer husky leaves removed
4 red chillies, deseeded
1 onion, finely chopped
6 cloves
1 tsp ground coriander
1 tsp ground cumin
1/2 tsp ground cinnamon
1/2 tsp ground black pepper
1/2 tsp ground turmeric
2 tbsp fish sauce

For the rendang
500g stewing or braising beef, cut into chunks
2 tbsp lime juice
1 tbsp soft dark brown sugar
400ml coconut milk
Jasmine rice, to serve

This is a lovely rich pie filling perfect for the autumnal season when game is as its best. Use venison, pheasant, rabbit, pigeon, partridge or any other game birds. You could also add venison or boar sausages if the cost of game is a little high. Some butchers sell a mixed selection of game meat by weight, which usually includes whatever happens to have been caught recently, saving on the preparation and cost of buying individual pieces.

Game Pie Filling

Serves 4

1 tbsp plain flour
1 tsp freshly ground
   black pepper
1/2 tsp salt
1.25–1.5kg mixed
   game, chopped into
   large chunks
1 red onion, coarsely
   chopped
150g mushrooms,
   quartered
2 smoked back bacon
   rashers, rinded and
   chopped
200ml red wine
200ml hot beef stock
1 tbsp red wine vinegar
1 bay leaf
500g packet of ready-
   made puff pastry
Fresh vegetables, to
   serve

1   Season the flour with the salt and pepper, coat the meat in the flour and place in the slow-cooker basin.

2   Add the chopped onion, quartered mushrooms and the chopped bacon to the basin and stir well.

3   Mix the wine and hot beef stock, then pour into the basin. Stir well.

4   Place the lid on tightly and cook on LOW for 6–8 hours until the meat is tender.

5   About half an hour before serving, following the preparation instructions on the puff pastry packaging, bake pieces of puff pastry to serve with your game and fresh vegetables.

This versatile recipe means you can either use it to fill a pie case that you have baked blind or just top with a baked piece of puff pastry (see page 189).

Steak and Ale Pie Filling

Serves 4

1 Put the flour, salt and pepper in the slow-cooker basin. Add the steak and the kidney, if using, and mix well, coating the steak with the flour.

2 Sprinkle the grated onion on top of the steak, add the chopped carrot and mix well.

3 Sprinkle the beef stock cubes into the ale and stir to dissolve. Pour into the basin along with the crushed garlic and the bay leaf.

4 Put the lid on and cook on LOW for 8–10 hours until the beef is tender.

2 tbsp plain flour
$\frac{1}{2}$ tsp salt
$\frac{1}{2}$ tsp ground black pepper
1.25kg stewing or braising steak, cut into chunks
200g pig or lamb kidneys, trimmed and diced (optional)
1 small onion, grated
1 small carrot, peeled and finely chopped
2 beef stock cubes
500ml ale or beer
1 garlic clove, crushed
1 bay leaf

A great way to use the leftover bones from a roast beef joint, the flavour that develops is fantastic and forms the perfect base for a soup or stew.

Beef Stock

Makes about 800ml stock

Approximately 2kg beef bones
2 celery sticks, finely chopped
1 carrot, peeled and finely chopped
1 large onion, finely chopped
2 garlic cloves, finely chopped
12 black peppercorns
1 tsp salt
750ml boiling water

1   Cut the beef bones as small as possible so that they fit into the slow-cooker basin.

2   Add all the vegetables. Add the spices and salt and pour over the boiling water.

3   Put the lid on tightly and cook on HIGH for 12–15 hours or overnight.

4   Cool, then refrigerate the stock. When cold, skim off the fat layer, then use the fresh stock within 3 days or warm slightly so that it liquefies and transfer to ice cube trays to freeze. Use within a month of freezing.

OPTION
Use lamb or pork bones instead of beef.

'Waste not want not' the saying goes and there is something satisfyingly frugal about have a roast chicken on Sunday, putting the carcass into the slow cooker on Sunday night and having fresh stock to use the following day to make soup, risotto or any of the other many recipes requiring chicken stock. You can start to experiment with flavours too, try adding a lemon grass stalk and a chilli for a Thai-style stock.

Chicken Stock

Makes 1–4 litres, depending on the size of your slow cooker

1   Break up the carcass and place in the slow-cooker basin, add the chopped vegetables, the herbs, garlic and peppercorns.

2   Cover with boiling water and cook on LOW for 10–12 hours.

3   When ready, allow to cool for about 15 minutes and then strain the stock into a bowl, cool and chill in the fridge. Use within 2 days or freeze and use within 1 month.

1 chicken carcass
1 onion, coarsely chopped
1 celery stick and tops, coarsely chopped
A few sprigs of fresh herbs, such as parsley, sage or thyme
1 garlic clove, crushed
12 peppercorns

Rhubarb and ginger are a classic combination and this lovely conserve means you'll be enjoying the rhubarb all year round. If you want more of a ginger kick, then add another teaspoon of ground ginger and a little more fresh grated ginger.

Rhubarb and Ginger Conserve

Makes about 4 jars (454g)

1kg fresh rhubarb, chopped into 1cm chunks
2 tsp ground ginger
30g freshly grated ginger
1kg jam sugar

1   Add the chopped rhubarb to the slow-cooker basin along with the rest of the ingredients and mix very well.

2   Put the lid on tightly and cook on HIGH for 30 minutes.

3   Stir well, then reduce the heat setting to LOW for 2 hours.

4   If you want to preserve this conserve in jars, it is best to do this whilst the conserve is still hot. You will need to scrupulously clean both the jars and lids, then sterilise the jars by putting them in a hot oven (preheated to 220°C) for about 15 minutes.

5   When you are ready to fill, remove the jars carefully from the oven and place on a tea towel. Using a small jug, scoop up the rhubarb conserve and pour into the jars, screw the lids on tightly and leave to cool.

Perfect for when there is a glut of cooking apples, make a batch and freeze portions or put into sterilized jars (see page 194) and use within a month. Using the cider option gives the sauce an extra zingy flavour.

Zingy Apple Sauce
Makes about 3 jars (454g)

1   Half fill the slow-cooker basin with cold water. Add the apples to the water as you prepare them to stop them from turning brown.

2   Drain off the cold water and sprinkle on the lemon juice. Add the sugar and water and stir.

3   Place the lid on tightly and cook on HIGH for 3–4 hours until you have a thick sauce.

OPTION
For chunky apple sauce, hold back 200g of the chopped apple and keep in cold water. In the last hour of cooking, stir in the retained apple. Leave to cook for the last hour.

1kg cooking apples, peeled, cored and chopped
1 tbsp lemon juice
100g sugar
100ml water or cider

Another perfect job for the slow cooker at Christmas, whilst you are busy with all the other elements of your festive meal, the slow cooking ensures a richness and depth of flavour that will be fabulous with your roast turkey.

Cranberry, Port and Orange Sauce

Makes about 600g

400g frozen or fresh cranberries
150ml port
100g soft light brown sugar
Grated zest of $1/2$ orange
Juice of 1 orange
1 tsp ground cinnamon

1   Combine all the ingredients in the slow cooker and mix well.

2   Place the lid on tightly and cook on LOW for 7–8 hours or on HIGH for 3–4 hours.

Making chutney in the slow cooker is such a breeze and it is very easy to adapt your recipes to suit your tastes or the ingredients you have a glut of in the garden. There are thousands of different recipes but if you keep to a few basic principles, you'll do a great job.

Chutney

Basic principles

- Vinegar and sugar are key to preserving the fruit and vegetables.

- Use red wine vinegar and dark sugars for a darker finish; use white wine vinegar or cider vinegar and white sugar for paler chutney.

- Use cooking apples as a base as these cook down to a translucent mush and give the chutney its smooth texture.

- In the slow cooker, there is no need to add extra liquid as there is enough in the apple, fruit and vegetables.

- Use whole spices as ground spices cloud the appearance of chutney and can be gritty.

- Dried fruit is a good way to get the deep caramelized flavours into the chutney. Raisins, dates and sultanas are the most popular. Pre-soak in fruit juice if you have time.

- Chutney needs to mature as the acidity is very harsh to start with, so make a few weeks in advance of when you want to use it.

- If you are putting the chutney into jars, make sure you scrupulously clean your jars and lids (a dishwasher is perfect) and then heat them in the oven to sterilize them both (see page 194). Always hot-fill the jars, don't let them cool.

- Use a jug to pour the chutney into the hot jars and put the lid on – don't tighten too much straight away. Let it cool and then tighten fully.

Basic recipe

1 Add the vinegar and sugar to the slow-cooker basin and switch on to HIGH. Stir until the sugar has dissolved.

2 Add the chopped apple and onion.

3 Add the chopped fruit and vegetables and stir well.

4 Add the spices and stir again.

5 Put the lid on tightly and cook on HIGH for 5–6 hours or until the chutney is a thick consistency.

OPTIONS
- Cranberry, orange and star anise
- Mango, onion seed and garlic
- Beetroot, cumin and ginger
- Green tomato and chilli

500ml vinegar
500g sugar
1kg cooking apples, such as Bramley, peeled, cored and chopped into 2cm pieces
1 large onion, finely chopped
1kg fruit, dried fruit and vegetables of your choice, chopped into 2cm pieces
2 tsp whole spices of your choice (or add crushed garlic, a cinnamon stick or a whole chilli)

A delicious winter warmer with a real spicy ginger kick, you can switch the slow cooker to KEEP WARM and use the slow cooker to serve this too.

Ginger and Orange Hot Toddy

Serves 4

1 litre ginger ale
1 orange
2cm piece of fresh root ginger, peeled and grated
1/2 cinnamon stick
50g sugar
100ml orange juice

1   Pour the ginger ale into the slow-cooker basin.

2   Zest the orange into the basin. Cut all the skin and pith off the orange and cut the flesh into chunks, removing any white core, and add the flesh to the basin.

3   Add the grated ginger, cinnamon, sugar and orange juice and stir well.

4   Put the lid on tightly and switch on to LOW for 3–4 hours.

5   When ready, serve warm. If you want to booze it up, add a shot of orange liqueur per serving.

This makes a lovely change to the festive mulled wine that we are all familiar with. Try to find a nice scrumpy cider for a rustic apple flavour.

Mulled Cider

Makes about 2 litres

2 litres cider
4 cloves
1 cinnamon stick
1 star anise
1 tsp vanilla
1 tsp mixed spice
2 tbsp sugar
1 apple, cored and sliced
1 orange, sliced
150ml orange liqueur

1 Pour the cider into the slow-cooker basin and add all the spices and the sugar.

2 Add the apple and orange slices. Stir in the liqueur.

3 Place the lid on tightly and warm on LOW for 3–4 hours. Turn down to the KEEP WARM setting to serve.

Index